NOW WHAT? I GOT A TAX NOTICE FROM THE IRS. HELP!

Defining and deconstructing the scary and confusing letters that land in your mailbox.

Jeffrey A. Schneider
EA, CTRS, NTPI Fellow

ISBN: 978-0692997154

Published by: SFS Tax Problem Publishing
Edited by: Jeffrey Schneider, EA, CTRS, NTPIF
Design and composition by: Jeffrey Schneider, EA, CTRS, NTPIF
Cover design by: Angie Alaya

Issued also as an eBook and Audio Book
Now What? I got a tax notice from the IRS. Help! is also available in e-book. The book is also available in audio versions by download, and download cards.

For ordering information or special discounts for bulk purchases, please contact:

Visit: http://nowwhathelp.com/ or http://igotataxnotice.com/ for more information.

Table of Contents
Life Saving Navigation

Dedication

I dedicate this book to my wife, my best friend and business partner, Ali. Without her encouragement and insight, I never would have been able to complete this endeavor. Having just gotten through my first book she is already planning my second book.
Thank you for being Lucy to my Ricky.

I love her dearly anyway and thank her from the bottom of my heart.

Acknowledgements

Thank you, Michael, ("The Roz Man") Rozbruch. You have not only been my teacher as I delved into the practical side of tax resolution, but my mentor. Michael, you have been nothing but encouraging and honest with your suggestions, opinions and forthcoming with your insights. I appreciate all of your patience and guidance. Without you my tax resolution practice would not be where it is today and where it will be tomorrow.

Thank you to all the many teachers and instructors that have given their time to teach me on everything representation over the years. There are too many to mention by name in this space, but many of you I consider a friend. You have inspired me to move ahead with tax representation. I have personally expressed my gratitude to you individually in the past, and I will continue to do so as I have continued to grow in this field.

Lastly, thank you, thank you, thank you, to Loren ("Weis Words") Weisman. In the beginning, our relationship was for branding, making 2-3 minute videos and a couple of podcasts. Since then, it turned into so much more.

Your humor, quick wit and imagination, took this "dry tax book" and all our branding efforts to a level that I never thought this

Enrolled Agent could reach when talking taxes. So again, thank you, Loren for all the hard work you put forth and all the effort you put into getting this book to press.

I now count you as a close friend, even though you are a Red Sox fan!

Foreword

How the best actions can be taken during the worst weather to allow for the right results.

The idea of receiving a letter from the IRS is not a pleasant one for anyone. What makes it worse is the confusion, the fear, the assumptions and the worst-case scenarios that can feel like a tidal wave of stress. Jeffrey Schneider is a rare professional that not only understands the intricacies of this world but also knows how to communicate in a way that allows for the best understanding of how the right actions can be taken during the worst weather to allow for the best results.

Not one to try to talk over some one's head, Schneider decompresses and defines the scary and not so scary in a language that anyone can understand and comprehend. There are plenty of tax professionals talking over your head and trying to impress; he is not that guy. He is the guy looking you dead in the eye and doing all he can to help you see every option. His goal with his clients is to clarify the situation, clear out the misconceptions and create the best plan and blueprint to remedy the situation.

In "Now What? I got a Tax Notice from the IRS. Help!" Jeff defines and deconstructs the scary and confusing letters in a fashion that mixes attention to detail with humor and an intricate clarification of what is what in the world of the IRS. This is not a book where Schneider tries to soften the punch or lighten the touch of the more severe letters. Certain letters are something to worry about, and it is repeatedly stressed that the attempt to go it alone is a terrible idea. Should that worst-case scenario occur though, hire Jeff or an enrolled agent with the right credentials to sail your ship correctly through the waters of trouble to find smoother seas.

Still, in other cases, Schneider identifies that many notices are nowhere near as life threatening as some might think and that the receiver of a letter has choices and some level of control. Jeffrey Schneider brings a maritime parallel to the world of the IRS and the storms that they can bring. With the right navigation, floatation and resuscitation devices, tools and tips, it is possible to stay alive and stay afloat regardless of how wild the waves, winds or weather can get.

Jeff Schneider captains a ship of knowledge that carries an array of life-preserving tax tips, quips, and advice that can prevent the worst-case scenarios from sinking your boat. This guide, this captain's log, this chart shares clear, understandable information you can easily sail through. Whether you have received a letter, fear that one is en route or want to know what could be in your future as well as a few preventative maintenance steps to avoid getting those letters, this book can benefit any taxpayer.

— Loren Weisman

Branding Strategist and Keynote Speaker

Author's Note

This book is down to earth, sometimes dry, but easy to digest guide to help you understand tax notices.

This is the guide to guide you after the letter or letters arrive and you ask yourself, Now What? Followed by Help!

"Now What, I got a tax notice from the IRS. Help!" identifies, explains and defines each letter or notice, the options you have and the next steps to take in order to get the help you need. From the common to the not so common notices, to what you can do about them and the different types of professionals as well as the different types of credentials that make the difference in correcting or resolving your specific situation.

With life preserving tips and sanity maintaining directions, this guide is your life preserver to hold on to while you read those notices that give you that sinking feeling.

So, when you get that notice, you don't have to panic, you don't have to drown in stress or worry and you will have a brief understanding of the best steps to achieve the best results as you head toward dry land.

Introduction

Pennies on the dollar

Anyone can save you pennies on the dollar when it comes to paying the IRS, it just depends upon how many pennies.

Third Party Designee	Do you want to allow another person to discuss this return with the IRS (see instructions)? ☐ **Yes.** Complete below. ☐ **No**		
	Designee's name ▶	Phone no. ▶	Personal identification number (PIN) ▶ ☐☐☐☐☐
Sign Here Joint return? See instructions. Keep a copy for your records.	Under penalties of perjury, I declare that I have examined this return and, to the best of my knowledge and belief, it is true, correct, and accurately lists all amounts and sources of income I received during the tax year. Declaration of preparer (other than the taxpayer) is based on all information of which the preparer has any knowledge.		
	Your signature	Date	Your occupation	Daytime phone number
	Spouse's signature. If a joint return. **both must sign.**	Date	Spouse's occupation	If the IRS sent you an Identity Protection PIN, enter it here (see inst.) ☐☐☐☐☐☐
Paid Preparer Use Only	Print/Type preparer's name	Preparer's signature	Date	Check ☐ if self-employed	PTIN
	Firm's name ▶		Firm's EIN ▶	
	Firm's address ▶		Phone no.	

"Under penalties of perjury, I disclose that I have examined the return and accompanying schedule and statements and to the best of my knowledge and belief, they are true, correct and accurately list all amounts and sources of income I received during the year."

You have seen this on every federal income tax form 1040, 1040A, or 1040EZ that you have ever filed. It means that you agree to be held responsible for all items on the return and affirm that you (and your spouse, if applicable) are reporting all of your income. Remember, all income is taxable, no matter where derived, unless specifically excluded.

This means that you need to report it all, including any income illegally obtained (remember Al Capone and his income tax evasion conviction) or anything received "under the table." If you have not noticed, the tax form does not mention expenses.

That does not mean that you should lie, but it does mean that the income portion of the form relates to the years when the Internal Revenue Service (IRS) can audit your return.

Under "normal circumstances" (when does a taxpayer think that getting an audit notice is normal? But I digress), the audit period is three years from the date you file your return or April 15th, whichever is later. The period is also called the three-year statute of limitations (SOL).

However, if you understate your income by more than 25%, the audit period or SOL is extended by another three years, for a total of six years. The law that mentions these SOLs does not say "expenses," but "understatement of income."

Now, if you purposefully lie about your expenses (or anything else, for that matter), that can be considered fraud, and there is no statute of limitations for fraud. So, let's assume for the remainder of this book that no one has acted fraudulently.

Now what does all this have to do with the purpose of this book?

Getting a notice from the IRS, when there are dollars involved, is tantamount to an audit. An audit does not only refer to an in-person meeting with a revenue agent or officer, but can also be by written communication.

In this book, we will discuss some of the most common notices (see the appendix for a complete list of notices and letters related to individuals), what you can do about them, and what your options are if the IRS says you owe them money and you do not have it.

We will also discuss, albeit briefly, the types of professional (credentialed or not) that are around and whether or not they can help in various situations. We will also lay out IRS processes and remedies (liens and levies) and detail how to respond. Finally, this book will discuss your options when you owe money and cannot pay within the timeframe required. These are called alternative collection options.

Now what is an EA, CTRS, NTPIF and Who Is Jeffrey A. Schneider?

I am an enrolled agent, or EA. As I will discuss in more detail later, an EA is the only federally licensed tax professional. I have been helping taxpayers like you file tax returns, respond to IRS notices, and solve their IRS debts for over 35 years. I have an undergraduate degree in finance and a master's degree in taxation. I worked for a time in Corporate America in addition to working various positions in private practice in different tax departments, culminating in a tax director position for a major jewelry retailer/wholesaler.

14

My practice, consisting of tax return preparation and taxpayer representation, is physically located on the Treasure Coast, on the southeast coast of Florida (with a satellite office in Palm Beach County), but I have clients all over the country.

In 2010, I became a fellow of the National Tax Practice Institute, a program of 72 credit hours provided by the National Association of Enrolled Agents. This program focuses solely on the many facets of representing taxpayers, individuals, and businesses before the IRS. In 2015, I passed an advanced exam offered by the American Society of Tax Problem Solvers to become a Certified Tax Resolution Specialist.

Over the years, I have given back to the profession through leadership at the local, state, and national levels. I have been president of two local chapters of the Florida Society of Enrolled Agents (FSEA), was elected president of the FSEA in 2013, and currently hold the title of director of the National Association of Enrolled Agents (NAEA), where I will complete my second two-year term in May 2018.

I was a founding and five-year member of the NAEA's Educating America Task Force, whose primary mission is to promote the EA credential and help individuals who prepare or want to prepare tax returns take the next step and become enrolled agents.

I have toured the country and put on webinars teaching other tax professionals, both licensed and not, about all things taxes, including practice and time management.

I also give presentations on taxes to other organizations and local governments.

After leaving New York in 1987 and Atlanta in 1990, I have been a Florida resident for the past 27 years. I live as a pseudo–empty nester in Port St. Lucie with my wife, Ali, and our two dogs, Boodah and PoPo.

The three administrative levels of the Internal Revenue Service are Audits, Collections and Appeals... oh my.

I became an enrolled agent so I am able to help all taxpayers in their dealings with all levels of the Internal Revenue Service.

Chapter 1

Let the buyer beware of credentials and the people they buy into.

To Be or Not To Be Licensed?

That is the question. Anyone can go into the tax preparation business. Technically, all you need (at the time of this publication) is a personal tax identification number (PTIN). While any business may or may not need a business license depending on their physical location, you do not need any professional license or credential to prepare taxes.

In the tax profession, there are only three total official credentials. One is the enrolled agent credential. The EA is the only authorized tax practitioner who has technical expertise in the field of taxation and who is empowered by the U.S. Department of the Treasury.

The Three Official Tax Credentials

In the tax profession, there are only three total official credentials. One is the enrolled agent credential. An enrolled agent (EA) is the only federally authorized tax practitioner who has technical expertise in the field of taxation and who is empowered by the U.S. Department of the Treasury to represent taxpayers before all administrative levels—examination, collection, and appeals—of the Internal Revenue Service (IRS).

An enrolled agent is a person who has earned the privilege of representing taxpayers before the IRS by either passing a three-part comprehensive IRS test called the Special Enrollment Examination, or SEE, covering individual and business tax returns, ethics, estates and trusts, and IRS practice and procedure.

Enrolled agent status is the highest credential the IRS awards.

Individuals who obtain this elite status must adhere to ethical standards and complete 72 hours of continuing education courses every three years.

The next credential is the certified public accountant (CPA). A certified public accountant has passed the CPA Exam and has been licensed by one of the 50 U.S. states (or one of five other jurisdictions). The CPA's license is renewed if the state's requirements, including maintaining continuing professional education credits, continue to be met.

To become a CPA, a person must do the following:

A) complete a college-level accounting program,

B) pass the Uniform CPA Examination, and

C) have a certain amount of professional work experience in accounting — typically, one year.

Once a person becomes a CPA, they can specialize in one specific area of finance or provide a wide range of services: corporate finance, taxes, financial and managerial accounting, or management consulting, just to name a few.

The last credential is the attorney/lawyer/esquire.

Tax attorneys are specialists in federal, state, and municipal rules and policies pertaining to tax liability and the process of taxation as it relates to estate transfers, material and intellectual property acquisitions, income from all sources, and business transactions of all kinds.

There are significant differences between the credentials.

Passing the bar or the CPA exam does not make someone a tax expert. All EAs are tax professionals, though some only prepare tax returns whereby some only represent clients before the IRS, while some (including your author) does both.

Professionals with any of the three credentials can represent clients at all administrative levels before the IRS; however, only those who pass the bar can go to court on behalf of a client. There is one exception to this: a special credential known as a U.S. Tax Court Practitioner (USTCP) that non-attorneys can achieve via exam.

This bi-annual test is one of the most difficult exams a tax professional can take, with only an 8-10% passing rate. Practitioners who pass this test are not attorneys, and are only allowed to practice before the tax court. Only attorneys can represent clients before the other courts, such as the Court of Appeals, District Court, the Court of Federal Claims, and of course, the U.S. Supreme Court.

The Annual Filing Season Program: Who are the other players?

There is a relatively new program called the Annual Filing Season Program. This is not a license or credential, but a voluntary program designed to have tax preparers take education in taxes, because you do not need a professional license or take any continuing education to prepare a tax return for compensation. In other words, it is not necessary to register for this or any program in order to prepare taxes for money. In general, to obtain an Annual Filing Season Program–Record of Completion, a return preparer must obtain 18 hours of continuing professional education credit from an IRS-approved continuing education provider. The hours must include a six-credit hour Annual Federal Tax Refresher (AFTR) course that covers filing season issues and tax law updates.

The IRS developed the Annual Filing Season Program in light of their loss in court in a case called "Loving vs. Commissioner," which dealt with whether the IRS overstepped its authority when it tried to regulate all tax return preparers. The IRS, through its Registered Tax Return Preparer program, required all preparers (who were not EAs, CPAs, or attorneys) of any tax return to take an exam, basically covering information on preparing individual taxes, and take continuing education courses.

A few preparers felt the IRS did not have the right to make them take a test or take continuing education course to prove minimal competency in taxes. So, they sued the IRS, and won. The IRS appealed, lost again, and decided not to ask the U.S. Supreme Court to rule. As such, we wait to see if Congress will intervene. And we wait. No intervention has occurred at the time of this writing. In any case, the Registered Tax Return Preparer program was abandoned, though the IRS was allowed to require tax preparers to have a Personal Taxpayer Identification Number or PTIN that can be used in lieu of the preparer's social security number. This is not, in any way, a substitute for a professional license or credential.

Although the IRS cannot now regulate tax return preparers, they can regulate representatives who practice before the IRS.

If you have a tax return prepared by a preparer that is not an EA, CPA, or lawyer (called unenrolled preparers), they can only help clients for whom they prepared the return, and only in relation to notices or an actual audit. If you do receive a notice on a self-prepared return and decide you need professional help, only an EA, CPA, or attorney (Circular 230 Practitioner) can represent you. The same goes for when you owe taxes that are now with the collections unit of the IRS. Your only choice for representation is to retain a Circular 230 Practitioner or handle it yourself.

Ask yourself: would you go to court in a civil lawsuit or for an injury claim?

I would hope not.

The same is true with taxes. Let the buyer beware – caveat emptor!!

Garbage in Garbage out.

An online tax program is only as good as the information the person enters into it and the understanding of what is being asked by the program.

Chapter 2

What can a tax professional do for you that an online program can't?

Should You Prepare Your Own Return?

As with many things in life, whether or not to file your own tax return depends. Cost is generally the deciding factor for the average person deciding whether to engage the services of a professional.

There are many alternatives to using a professional. You can use the off the shelf software, like Turbo Tax or Tax Act, to name a couple.

But these programs, like the off-the-shelf accounting programs, are only as good as the person using it and the information entered. These programs do ask a series of questions, but they only go so far.

They cannot probe
the taxpayer for answers.

Seek professional assistance instead of preparing the return yourself in the following situations:

1) Sales of investments (stocks, bonds, or mutual funds)

2) Refinancing a home where there are closing costs, including origination fees

3) Refinancing a home or securing a home equity loan where the loan exceeds the original purchase (plus improvements) and where the mortgage balances are over $1 million

4) Having more than two mortgages or homes

5) Taking a distribution from a retirement account under extenuating circumstances when under age 59½

6) Moving from one location to another

7) Having monies withheld from a paycheck for child care

8) Having earnings from working out of the country

9) Gambling activity, including the following:

   a. Receiving a W-2G

   b. Winning a prize

10) Winning a lawsuit that includes being awarded legal fees

11) Employee expenses that were not reimbursed by your employer

12) Being involved in a business (self-proprietorship, S-corporation or partnership) in any of the following capacities:

   a. Materially and actively involved

   b. Hobby activity

   c. Investment

13) Having rental properties, including the following:

   a. Personal single residence

   b. Multi-unit residence

   c. Part-time vacation home

   d. Commercial property

   e. Boarder

   f. Short-term rental

14) Having casualty or theft

15) A change in life circumstances, including the following:

   a. Divorce. Questions to consider include:

      i. Who will have custody of any children?

      ii. Who does the child or children live with?

      iii. Are you receiving or paying alimony and/or child support?

b. Death of a loved one, especially if there are significant assets

16) Giving gifts that exceed $14,000 to any one person during the year

17) Receiving private or public disability payments, including workers' compensation benefits and lump sum payments

18) High charitable contributions

a. Cash, checks or charges greater than $5,000

b. Items of property

19) Having investment expenses

20) Having education costs, including the following:

a. College or university

b. Distributions from a §529 or other tuition prepaid plan

c. Scholarships

21) Taking care of a parent

22) Providing support for an individual other than a child

23) Bartering activity

24) Incurring out-of-pocket costs from teaching

25) High medical expenses, especially if you are self-employed or the shareholder of an S-corporation

26) Having a mortgage with an individual versus a bank or mortgage company

Online tax programs do not get to know their clients.

Chapter 3

The Role of the Taxpayer,
The Representative, and the IRS

The victim, the hero and... them.

Taxpayer Role

This role is easy, as that is you.

Whether you prepare your own return or use a professional (licensed or otherwise), you are to report your income, expenses, and deductions as accurately as possible and take positions that can be reasonably defended. That does not mean you will win your argument, but breaking this down to the basics, you should only make claims if you have a reasonable basis to believe you'll win.

In tax controversies, who represents you can be the whole ballgame. "Tax controversy" is a term or art meaning a contested matter before the IRS, state or local government, civil or criminal, administrative or judicial.

The taxpayer, you, has a legal responsibility to report your income from all sources. As I mentioned in the preface, this includes legal and illegal sources.

Al Capone is the most well-known convict whose failure to report illegal income landed him in jail.

The legal authorities could not convict Capone for his illegal activities. How did they convict him? Tax evasion! They found out that he did not report the ill-gotten gains from his illegal activities. They could not prove that he received this income from illegal sources, but they were able to prove he had income and did not report it on a tax return and pay his taxes.

Many people believe that if they did not get a tax form (usually a 1099), they do not have to report the income. That is so far from the truth. Let me give you an example.

You are an independent contractor, in business for yourself, providing services (selling a product does not warrant a 1099-MISC) to businesses.

However, there is a dollar floor where the businesses you contract with do not have to issue a 1099-MISC to an individual service provider or the IRS. That floor is $600 or less. Let us assume that you work for 100 different businesses and earn $590 from each.

Each of these businesses, since you made $600 or less, will not, because they are not required to, send out the form to you or the IRS. Do you still have to report the $59,000 of income? Of course you do.

In a worst-case scenario, say you earned $5,900 from each of these businesses and you did not get the 1099. If you take the position that you only report the earning listed on forms you have received, how do you know the IRS did not get their copy and yours was lost in the mail? You don't. You file a return missing some income and you will get a notice called a CP2000. We will discuss this and other notices in chapter 6.

The same thing happens with bank interest from savings or checking accounts. If you earn more than $10 in interest in a year, the bank should send out a 1099-INT. In these times of miniscule returns, many people earn less than $10 on their savings or checking accounts from each account each year. As such, they do not receive a 1099-INT or does the bank or financial institution send one to the IRS. Are you required to report this income anyway? You should now know the answer to this question. (It's yes, in case you do not get my drift.)

The Representative

Your tax preparer can only report the information you give them, but there is a certain required due diligence that a reputable preparer, licensed or otherwise, must and should conduct. In this exercise, the preparer asks the taxpayer(s) questions about a wide range of issues. In addition to questions, written or verbal, the preparer will request back-up documentation. Documenting your income and deductions is paramount to defending what is put on the return.

There are many unscrupulous preparers.

These individuals can be EAs, CPAs, attorneys, or unlicensed preparers. It is not the license but the person. In my practice, I sometimes lose as many potential new clients each and every tax season. They come in and leave when I start to ask my questions. They say to me...

"My last preparer never asked me this."

When I inform a client that this is part of my due diligence, they tend to get up and leave. Preparers, especially licensed preparers, have certain professional ethics we have to abide by. Lying, exaggerating, or just putting anything a client requests on a return is not abiding by these ethical standards. Each professional credential is required to take a certain number of ethics hours in their continuing education. An enrolled agent, for example, has to take two hours *every year*.

All licensed tax professionals have to adhere to, what is known as Circular 230. It is a long and detailed set of rules that we have to follow.

The important thing to remember is that although the professional is responsible for what goes on a return, it is still your return. Remember that perjury statement in the introduction?

Penalties can be high for lying.

They can be up to 100% of the tax (and let's not get into the criminal aspect).

That is not to say that the preparer does not have some responsibility. Preparers are to report all the information provided to them. The law does say that preparers are not to audit the taxpayer when they provide information, either verbally or in writing; however, they are not to put their heads in the sand, either. That is the due diligence I was referring to.

Under a law passed in 2010 that took effect starting with 2016 returns, certain documentation is to be provided for all returns that include the earned income tax credit, the child tax credit, and/or the American Opportunity (Education) Tax Credit. Taxpayers have to provide documentation regarding their dependents. If preparers do not ask for and receive this, they can be subject to penalties.

These credits are known as "refundable credits," which means that even when a taxpayer owes no income tax, they can get a refund.

There are many fraudulent returns where these credits are concerned. The IRS wants questions asked, and they have a form (8867) that has to be completed for every return with one or more of the credits. So, when you are asked these questions, please do not *"shoot the messenger."*

IRS Role

The IRS plays a significant role in all of this as well. Their role can be electronic (via automated notices like the CP2000) or face-to-face (through an audit). There is one thing you have to understand, and there are no if, ands, or buts about it:

The IRS is not looking out for any aspect of your best interest. They are a government agency.

They are the world's largest collection agency.

Have you ever received a call from a collection agency? The recording says, "This call is being recorded, and anything said on this call will be used in the collection of a debt." The IRS does not come out and say this, but rest assured, they are doing the same. When you call IRS customer service, they will try to help answer a question, and most are friendly and courteous, but do not mistake them for being a friend.

Taking into account the current continual decrease in the funding of the Service by Congress, employees of the IRS are neither the most experienced of tax professionals nor the most knowledgeable.

Sometimes, you may know more than they do.

As the saying goes, "Let the buyer beware" when they call the main IRS customer service number (1-800-829-1040)."

The IRS, like most businesses, has a mission statement.

"Provide America's taxpayers top quality service by helping them understand and meet their tax responsibilities and enforce the law with integrity and fairness to all.

This mission statement describes our role and the public's expectation about how we should perform that role.

- *In the United States, the Congress passes tax laws and requires taxpayers to comply.*

- *The taxpayer's role is to understand and meet his or her tax obligations.*

- *The IRS role is to help the large majority of compliant taxpayers with the tax law, while ensuring that the minority who are unwilling to comply pay their fair share."*

Nowhere does it say, "help the taxpayer pay the lowest tax"; just their fair share.

It is the definition of "fair share" that is the crux of most IRS versus taxpayer controversy.

Most taxpayers do not realize that they have the right to be represented when it comes to dealing with the IRS.

Do not deal with the IRS alone.
You do not have to go it alone and you do not need a lawyer.

This is a major misconception from many that find themselves in deep waters with the IRS.

Chapter 4

The protection and fundamental rights you have with the IRS

The Taxpayers Bill of Rights

We all know that Thomas Jefferson wrote the U.S. Bill of Rights. But did you know that as a taxpayer, you have your own Bill of Rights? The IRS has adopted a Taxpayer Bill of Rights, as proposed by National Taxpayer Advocate Nina Olson. It applies to all taxpayers in their dealings with the IRS. The Taxpayer Bill of Rights groups the existing rights in the tax code into 10 fundamental rights, and makes them clear, understandable, and accessible.

The Right to Be Informed

Taxpayers have the right to know what they need to do to comply with tax laws. They are entitled to clear explanations of the law and IRS procedures in all tax forms, instructions, publications, notices, and correspondence. They have the right to be informed of

IRS decisions about their tax accounts and to receive clear explanations of the outcomes.

Now What This Means for You

- If you receive a notice fully or partially disallowing your refund claim, including a refund you claim on your income tax return, it must explain the specific reasons why the claim is being disallowed.

- Generally, if you owe a penalty, each written notice of such penalty must provide an explanation of the penalty, including the name of the penalty, the authority under the Internal Revenue Code, and how it is calculated.

- During an in-person interview with the IRS as part of an audit, the IRS employee must explain the audit process and your rights under that process. Likewise, during an in-person interview with the IRS concerning the collection of your tax, the IRS employee must explain the collection process and your rights under that process. Generally, the IRS uses Publication 1, *Your Rights as a Taxpayer,* to meet this requirement.

- The IRS must include on certain notices the amount (if any) of the tax, interest, and certain penalties you owe and must explain why you owe these amounts.

- The IRS must inform you in certain publications and instructions that when you file a joint income tax return with your spouse, both of you are responsible for all tax due and any additional amounts due for that tax year, unless "innocent spouse" relief applies.

- The IRS must inform you in Publication 1, *Your Rights as a Taxpayer*, and all collection-related notices that in certain circumstances, you may be relieved of all or part of the tax owed with your joint return.

This is sometimes referred to as "innocent spouse relief."

- The IRS must explain in Publication 1, *Your Rights as a Taxpayer*, how it selects which taxpayers will be audited.

- If the IRS proposes to assess tax against you, it will send you a letter providing the examination report, stating the proposed changes, and providing you with the opportunity for a review by an appeals officer if you respond, generally within 30 days. This letter, which in some cases is the first communication from the examiner, must provide an explanation of the entire process from examination (audit) through collection and explain that the Taxpayer Advocate Service may be able to assist you. Generally, Publication 3498, *The Examination Process*, or Publication 3498-A, *The Examination Process (Audits by Mail)*, is included with this letter.

- If you enter into a payment plan, known as an installment agreement, the IRS must send you an annual statement that provides how much you owe at the beginning of the year, how much you paid during the year, and how much you still owe at the end of the year.

- You have the right to access certain IRS records, including instructions and manuals to staff, unless such records are required or permitted to be withheld under the Internal Revenue Code, the Freedom of Information Act, or the Privacy Act. Certain IRS records must be available to you electronically.

- If the IRS is proposing to adjust the amount of tax you owe, you will typically be sent a statutory notice of deficiency, which informs you of the proposed change. This notice provides you with a right to challenge the proposed adjustment in Tax Court without first paying the proposed adjustment.

  To exercise this right, you must file a petition with the Tax Court within 90 days of the date of the notice being sent (or 150 days if the address on the notice is outside the United States or if you are out of the country at the time the notice is mailed). Thus, the statutory notice of deficiency is your ticket to Tax Court.

The Right to Quality Service

Taxpayers have the right to receive prompt, courteous, and professional assistance in their dealings with the IRS, to be spoken to in a way they can easily understand, to receive clear and easily understandable communications from the IRS, and to have a way to file complaints about inadequate service.

Now What This Means for You

- The IRS must include information about your right to Taxpayer Advocate Service (TAS) assistance, and how to contact TAS, in all notices of deficiency.

- When collecting tax, the IRS should treat you with courtesy. Generally, the IRS should only contact you between 8 a.m. and 9 p.m. The IRS should not contact you at your place of employment if the IRS knows or has reason to know that your employer does not allow such contacts.

- If you are an individual taxpayer eligible for Low Income Taxpayer Clinic (LITC) assistance (generally, if your income is at or below 250% of the federal poverty level), the IRS may provide information to you about your eligibility for assistance from an LITC.

  o For more information, see IRS Publication 4134, *Low Income Taxpayer Clinic List*, or find an LITC near you.

- Certain notices written by the IRS must contain the name, phone number, and identifying number of the IRS employee, and all notices must include a telephone number that you may contact. During a phone call or in-person interview, the IRS employee must provide you with his or her name and ID number.

- The IRS is required to publish the local address and phone number of the IRS in local phone books.

The Right to Pay No More Than the Correct Amount of Tax

Taxpayers have the right to pay only the amount of tax legally due and to have the IRS apply all tax payments properly.

Now What This Means for You

- If the IRS is proposing to adjust the amount of tax you owe, you will typically be sent a statutory notice of deficiency, which informs you of the proposed change. This notice provides you with a right to challenge the proposed adjustment in Tax Court without first paying the proposed adjustment.

To exercise this right, you must file a petition with the Tax Court within 90 days of the date of the notice being sent (or 150 days if the address on the notice is outside the United States or if you are out of the country at the time the notice is mailed). Thus, the statutory notice of deficiency is your ticket to Tax Court.

- If you are an individual taxpayer eligible for LITC assistance (generally, if your income is at or below 250% of the federal poverty level), the IRS may provide information to you about your eligibility for assistance from an LITC.

    o For more information, see IRS Publication 4134, *Low Income Taxpayer Clinic List*, or find an LITC near you.

- If you believe you have overpaid your taxes, you can file a refund claim asking for the money back, within certain time limits.

- You may request that any amount owed be removed if it exceeds the correct amount due under the law, if the IRS has assessed it after the period allowed by law, or if the assessment was done in error or violation of the law.

- You may request that the IRS remove any interest from your account that was caused by the IRS's unreasonable errors or delays. For example, if the IRS delays issuing a statutory notice of deficiency because the assigned employee was away for several months attending training, and interest accrues during this time, the IRS may abate the interest as a result of the delay (*IRC § 6404(e)*).

- If you have a legitimate doubt that you owe part or all of the tax debt, you can submit a settlement offer called an Offer in Compromise—Doubt as to Liability offer using Form 656-L.

- You will receive an annual notice from the IRS stating the amount of the tax due, which will help you check that all payments you made were received and correctly applied.

- If you enter into a payment plan, known as an installment agreement, the IRS must send you an annual statement that provides how much you owe at the beginning of the year, how much you paid during the year, and how much you still owe at the end of the year.

The Right to Appeal an IRS Decision in an Independent Forum

Taxpayers are entitled to a fair and impartial administrative appeal of most IRS decisions, including many penalties, and have the right to receive a written response regarding the Office of Appeals' decision. Taxpayers generally have the right to take their cases to court.

Now What This Means for You

- The Commissioner must ensure an independent IRS Office of Appeals that is separate from the IRS Office that initially reviewed your case. Generally, Appeals cannot discuss a case with the IRS unless you or your representative is given the opportunity to be present.

- The IRS must ensure that an appeals officer is regularly available within each state.

- If you do not agree with the proposed adjustment as a result of an examination (audit), you have the right to an administrative appeal.

- In certain situations, a taxpayer has the opportunity to request a conference with the Office of Appeals.

- You have the right to request an independent review conducted by the Office of Appeals prior to the termination of your installment agreement.

- If the IRS is proposing to adjust the amount of tax you owe, you will typically be sent a statutory notice of deficiency, which informs you of the proposed change. This notice provides you with a right to challenge the proposed adjustment in Tax Court without first paying the proposed adjustment. Thus, the statutory notice of deficiency is your ticket to Tax Court.

- To exercise your right to challenge the proposed adjustment in Tax Court *without* first paying the proposed adjustment, you must file a petition with the Tax Court within 90 days of the date of the notice being sent (or 150 days if the address on the notice is outside the United States or if you are out of the country at the time the notice is mailed).

- In certain circumstances, the Office of Appeals has exclusive authority to settle your case. Generally, for the four months after you petition Tax Court, Appeals will be the only office within the IRS that can settle your case as long as the statutory notice of deficiency or other notice of determination was not issued by Appeals.

- Generally, you are entitled to request a Collection Due Process hearing to dispute the first proposed levy action relating to a particular tax liability. The independent IRS appeals or settlement officer conducting your hearing must have no prior involvement with the taxes the IRS is attempting to collect. If you disagree with the hearing officer's determination, you can challenge it in Tax Court.

- If the IRS rejects your request for an offer in compromise asking the IRS to settle your tax debt for less than the amount owed, or a payment plan called an installment agreement, then you may seek an independent review of the rejection with the IRS Office of Appeals.

- You can generally request that an issue you have not been able to resolve with the IRS examination or collection division be transferred to the Office of Appeals. For issues that are unresolved after working with Appeals, you may request non-binding mediation (where a neutral third party will help you try to reach a settlement) or binding arbitration (where you and the IRS will be bound by a third party's decision). You may also request non-binding mediation or arbitration after unsuccessfully trying to enter into a closing agreement or offer in compromise.

- Generally, if you have fully paid the tax and your tax refund claim is denied or if no action is taken on the claim within six months, then you may file a refund suit in a United States District Court or the United States Court of Federal Claims.

- In very limited circumstances, you can ask a court to make a determination on certain tax issues prior to there being an actual dispute between you and the IRS. For example, a court may be able to determine whether an organization is tax-exempt or if a retirement plan is valid.

- A jeopardy levy or assessment allows the IRS, in very limited circumstances, to bypass normal administrative safeguards and protections. For example, the IRS may issue a jeopardy levy if the IRS has knowledge that the taxpayer is fleeing the country. If the IRS makes such a jeopardy levy or assessment, you have the right to file a lawsuit, and the court will determine whether the levy or assessment was reasonable under the circumstances and whether the amount is appropriate.

The Right to Privacy

Taxpayers have the right to expect that any IRS inquiry, examination, or enforcement action will comply with the law and be no more intrusive than necessary, and will respect all due process rights, including search and seizure protections and a Collection Due Process hearing where applicable.

Now What This Means for You

- During a Collection Due Process hearing, an independent IRS appeals or settlement officer must consider whether the IRS's lien filing balances the government's need for the efficient collection of taxes with your legitimate concern that the IRS's collection actions are no more intrusive than necessary.

- During a Collection Due Process hearing, an independent IRS appeals or settlement officer must consider whether the IRS's proposed levy action balances the government's need for the efficient collection of taxes with your legitimate concern that the IRS's collection actions are no more intrusive than necessary.

- The IRS cannot levy any of your personal property in the following situations: before it sends you a notice of demand, while you have a request for a payment plan pending, and if the IRS will not recover any money from seizing and selling your property.

- The IRS cannot seize certain personal items, such as

o necessary schoolbooks,

o clothing,

o undelivered mail,

o certain amounts of furniture and household items,

o and tools of a trade.

- There are limits on the amount of wages that the IRS can levy (seize) in order to collect tax that you owe. A portion of wages equivalent to the standard deduction combined with any deductions for personal exemptions is protected from levy.

- The IRS cannot seize your personal residence, including a residence used as a principal residence by your spouse, former spouse, or minor child, without first getting court approval, and it must show there is no reasonable alternative for collecting the tax debt from you.

- The revenue officer must attempt to personally contact you, and if you indicate the seizure would cause a hardship, he or she must at least assist you in contacting the Taxpayer Advocate Service, if not provide the requested relief.

- The IRS issued interim guidance that extends these protections to suits to foreclose a lien on a principal residence. According to this guidance, the IRS should not pursue a suit to foreclose a lien on your principal residence unless it has considered hardship issues and there are no reasonable administrative remedies.

- As soon as practicable after seizure, the IRS must provide written notice to the owner of the property that the property will be put up for sale. Before the sale of the property, the IRS shall determine a minimum bid price. Before the property is sold, if the owner of the property pays the amount of the tax liability plus the expenses associated with the seizure, the IRS will return the property to the owner.

- Within 180 days after the sale, any person having an interest in the property may redeem the property sold by paying the amount the purchaser paid plus interest.

- If the IRS sells your property, you will receive a breakdown of how the money received from the sale of your property was applied to your tax debt.

- Under §3421 of the Restructuring and Reform Act of 1998, IRS employees are required, "where appropriate," to seek approval by a supervisor prior to filing a Notice of Federal Tax Lien. Section 3421 further requires that disciplinary actions be taken when such approval is not obtained.

- The IRS should not seek intrusive and extraneous information about your lifestyle during an audit if there is no reasonable indication that you have unreported income.

- If you submit an offer to settle your tax debt, and the offer relates only to how much you owe (known as a "doubt as to liability offer in compromise"), you do not need to submit any financial documentation.

The Right to Confidentiality

Taxpayers have the right to expect that any information they provide to the IRS will not be disclosed unless authorized by the taxpayer or by law. Taxpayers have the right to expect the IRS to investigate and take appropriate action against its employees, return preparers, and others who wrongfully use or disclose taxpayer return information.

Now What This Means for You

- In general, the IRS may not disclose your tax information to third parties unless you give it permission, *e.g.*, you request that the preparer disclose information in connection with a mortgage or student loan application.

- If a tax return preparer discloses or uses your tax information for any purpose other than for tax preparation, the preparer may be subject to civil penalties. If the disclosure or improper use is done knowingly or recklessly, the preparer may also be subject to criminal fines and imprisonment.

- Communications between you and an attorney with respect to legal advice the attorney gives you are generally privileged. A similar privilege applies to tax advice you receive from an individual who is authorized to practice before the IRS (*e.g.*, certified public accountant, enrolled agent, and enrolled actuary), but only to the extent that the communication between you and that individual would be privileged if it had been between you and an attorney.

  o For example, communication between you and an individual authorized to practice before the IRS regarding the preparation of a tax return is not privileged because there would be no similar privilege between a taxpayer and an attorney. The privilege relating to taxpayer communications with an individual authorized to practice before the IRS only applies in the contexts of noncriminal tax matters before the IRS and noncriminal tax proceedings in federal court where the United States is a party.

- In general, the IRS cannot contact third parties, *e.g.*, your employer, neighbors, or bank, to obtain information about adjusting or collecting your tax liability unless it provides you with reasonable notice in advance. Subject to some exceptions, the IRS is required to periodically provide you a list of the third-party contacts and upon request.

- The National Taxpayer Advocate and Local Taxpayer Advocates may decide whether to share with the IRS any information you (or your representative) provide them regarding your tax matter, including the fact that you've contacted the Taxpayer Advocate Service.

The Right to Retain Representation

Taxpayers have the right to retain an authorized representative of their choice to represent them in their dealings with the IRS. Taxpayers have the right to be told that if they cannot afford to hire a representative, they may be eligible for assistance from a Low Income Taxpayer Clinic.

Now What This Means for You

- If you have won your case in court, under certain conditions, you may be entitled to recover certain reasonable administrative and litigation costs related to your dispute with the IRS.

In most situations, the IRS must suspend an interview if you request to consult with a representative, such as an attorney, CPA, or enrolled agent.

- You may select a person, such as an attorney, CPA, or EA, to represent you in an interview with the IRS. The IRS cannot require that you attend with your representative, unless it formally summons you to appear.

- If you are an individual taxpayer eligible for LITC assistance (generally, your income must be at or below 250% of the federal poverty level to be eligible), you may ask an LITC to represent you (for free or a minimal fee) in your tax dispute before the IRS or federal court.

The Right to a Fair and Just Tax System

Taxpayers have the right to expect the tax system to consider facts and circumstances that might affect their underlying liabilities, ability to pay, or ability to provide information timely. Taxpayers have the right to receive assistance from the Taxpayer Advocate Service if they are experiencing financial difficulty or if the IRS has not resolved their tax issues properly and timely through its normal channels.

Now What This Means for You

- If you cannot pay your tax debt in full and you meet certain conditions, you can enter into a payment plan with the IRS where you pay a set amount over time, generally on a monthly basis.

- You may request that any amount owed be eliminated if it exceeds the correct amount due under the law, if the IRS has assessed it after the period allowed by law, or if the assessment was done in error or violation of the law.

- You may request that the IRS remove any interest from your account that was caused by the IRS's unreasonable errors or delays. For example, if the IRS delays issuing a statutory notice of deficiency because the assigned employee was away for several months attending training, and interest accrues during this time, the IRS may abate the interest as a result of the delay.

The time limit for asking for the taxes you paid to be refunded may be suspended during a time you are unable to manage your financial affairs due to a mental or physical health problem.

- If you have acted with reasonable care you may be entitled to relief from certain penalties. Additionally, if you have a reasonable basis for taking a particular tax position, such as a position on your return or a claim for refund, you may be entitled to relief from certain penalties. Reliance on the advice of a tax professional can in certain circumstances represent reasonable cause for the abatement of certain penalties.

- If you use a return preparer who takes an unreasonable or reckless position that results in underreporting your tax, that preparer may be subject to penalties.

- You can submit an offer in compromise asking the IRS to settle your tax debt for less than the full amount if 1) you believe you do not owe all or part of the tax debt, 2) you are unable to pay all of the tax debt within the time permitted by law to collect, or 3) there are factors such as equity, hardship, or public policy that you think the IRS should consider in determining whether to compromise your liability.

If you are experiencing a significant hardship because of IRS action or inaction, you may be eligible for assistance from the Taxpayer Advocate Service (TAS).

- A significant hardship occurs when a tax problem causes you financial difficulties or you have been unable to resolve your problem through normal IRS channels. You may also be eligible if you believe an IRS system or procedure isn't working as it should *(IRC § 7803(c))*.

- You have the right to request that the Taxpayer Advocate Service issue a Taxpayer Assistance Order (TAO) on your behalf if you are experiencing a significant hardship. TAS can issue a TAO ordering the IRS to take certain actions, cease certain actions or refrain from taking certain actions, and it can also order the IRS to reconsider, raise to a higher level, or speed up an action.

- If you are trying to settle your tax debt with an offer in compromise based on your inability to pay, the IRS considers your income, assets, and expenses in deciding whether to accept your offer. Generally, the IRS uses guidelines for standard allowances for cost of living expenses, unless you will not able to pay your basic living expenses. Then, the IRS must consider your actual expenses. If you are offering to settle because you believe you don't owe the tax liability, you will not need to submit financial information.

- If you are a low-income taxpayer trying to settle your tax debt with an offer in compromise, the IRS cannot reject your offer solely on the basis of the amount offer. For example, it cannot reject an offer solely because the amount offered is so low it does not cover the IRS costs for processing the offer.

- If you submit an offer to settle your tax debt, and the offer relates only to how much you owe (a "doubt as to liability offer in compromise"), the IRS cannot reject your offer solely because it cannot locate your tax return to verify how much you owe.

- The IRS cannot levy (seize) all of your wages to collect your unpaid tax. A portion will be exempt from levy to allow you to pay basic living expenses.

- The IRS must release all or part of a levy and notify the person upon whom the levy was made if one of the following situations exist:

  1. the underlying liability is satisfied or becomes unenforceable due to the lapse of time,

  2. the taxpayer enters into an installment agreement, unless the agreement specifies otherwise,

  3. the release of the levy will facilitate collection of liability,

  4. the IRS determines the levy is creating an economic hardship for the taxpayer, or

  5. the fair market value of the property levied is greater than the liability and releasing the levy on part of the property would not impair collection of the underlying liability.

- If you are an individual taxpayer eligible for LITC assistance (generally, your income must be at or below 250% of the federal poverty level guidelines to be eligible), you have the right to seek assistance from an LITC to ensure that the IRS is considering your particular facts and circumstances.

- If the IRS is proposing to adjust the amount of tax you owe, you will typically be sent a statutory notice of deficiency, which informs you of the proposed change. This notice provides you with a right to challenge the proposed adjustment in Tax Court without first paying the proposed adjustment. To exercise this right, you must file a petition with the Tax Court within 90 days of the date of the notice being sent (or 150 days if the address on the notice is outside the United States or if you are out of the country at the time the notice is mailed). Thus, the statutory notice of deficiency is your ticket to Tax Court.

The Taxpayer Advocate's Service

There are times that even an experienced representative runs into an administrative roadblock. What can one do? Well, we have mentioned the Taxpayer Advocate Service (TAS) several times in writing about the Taxpayer's Bill of Rights. This agency is part of the IRS, but it is totally separate and autonomous.

Now What Is TAS and what can the TAS do for Us?

The Taxpayer Advocate Service works by helping taxpayers with individual problems and by recommending "big picture" or systemic changes at the IRS or in the tax laws.

Their job is to ensure that every taxpayer is treated fairly and that you know and understand your rights. As an independent organization within the IRS, they protect taxpayers' rights under the Taxpayer Bill of Rights, help taxpayers resolve problems with the IRS, and recommend changes that will prevent the problems.

Systemic Help

Some of the problems we deal with are not limited to a single taxpayer. The TAS looks at patterns in taxpayer issues to determine if an IRS process or procedure is causing a problem, and if so, to recommend steps to resolve the problem.

Each year, the National Taxpayer Advocate presents an annual report to Congress, identifying at least 20 of the most serious problems facing taxpayers. In recent years, the key issues in the report have included tax-related identity theft, fraud by certain tax return preparers, and the need for a Taxpayer Bill of Rights (which the IRS has adopted.)

Individual Help

If you are having a tax problem that you haven't been able to resolve on your own, advocates may be able to help. You may be eligible for help if your IRS problem is causing financial difficulty or if you believe an IRS procedure just isn't working as it should.

The TAS has offices in every state, the District of Columbia, and Puerto Rico, but not in every city. If you qualify for help, you will be assigned to one advocate who will work with the IRS, for free, to get your problems resolved.

If you receive a 'certified' message in a bottle with an audit notice, be sure to have the most complete records and do not forget those receipts before the IRS boards your vessel for inspection.

Chapter 5

The best steps to take in order to avoid an audit.

Due Diligence and doing it the right way the first time.

An audit is an examination conducted by the IRS (or a state or local government) to verify that the information reported on the return was accurate.

Most honest (and many not-so-honest) taxpayers dread seeing a certified letter from the IRS. If they do not, to the best of their knowledge, owe the IRS back taxes, the letter is in most cases related to an audit summons.

The question a lot of taxpayers ask is…

"How much can I deduct not to be audited?"

There is no such formula. The IRS chooses what returns are to be audit in a variety of ways, which are discussed below. To be honest, less than 1% of all returns are audited. The percentage increases when it comes to correspondence audits.

Now What Are The Types of Audits?

There are four types of IRS audits, and you will prepare differently for each one.

1. Correspondence Audit

This is the least severe type of audit, and involves the IRS sending a letter in the mail requesting more information about part of a tax return. For instance, the agency may have questions regarding your charitable deductions and request you send in receipts to substantiate your deduction.

If you have all the documentation to back up the deduction, send it in to the IRS, and you should be fine. If you feel that you may not have everything or if you're unsure, you should seek professional help. Recall Chapters 2 and 3 on your options for professional assistance.

If you self-prepared the return, you can only be represented by an EA, CPA, or attorney. An unlicensed preparer cannot represent a taxpayer for any reason on a return that they did not themselves prepare.

2. Office Audit

If the IRS has more questions about your return, then you'll get a letter in the mail inviting you into an IRS office for the audit. The office audit is more serious. You may want your tax preparer to come with you. For any return that I prepare, I stress that no client goes to visit the auditor.

Treat the situation like a trial: You, in most circumstances, would not represent yourself in court.

You go with a lawyer. The same is true of an office audit. You know the saying, "A client who represents themselves has a fool for a client". You should hire an experienced EA or CPA to represent your best interests.

Some professionals say that the preparer of the return should not represent you in an audit. That may be true if there are controversial positions represented on a return (*i.e.*, tax shelters). Why? Because if there is an intimation of fraud, the taxpayer and the preparer will throw each other under the bus. Just some food for thought.

In any case, most office audits are done within a few hours. Unless the preparer needs to present other items that the auditor is asking for, the audit rarely lasts more than one day.

3. Field Audit

This is the most serious type of audit, and involves the IRS visiting you at your home or office. It is usually related to an audit of a business, be it a partnership an incorporated entity or if you are sole-proprietorship (limited liability company or not). The field audit is more serious because the IRS auditor looks to see if s/he needs to ask for explanation of certain other things (inventory, equipment, and so on). They don't want to limit their request to particular items as it is noted on the return. The auditor will make a written, formal Information Document Request or IDR.

However, these things can and usually do change once they see the place of business. While there are far fewer field audits than office or correspondence audits, going it alone for a field audit will be hazardous to the financial health of the taxpayer due to their more serious nature.

First, no matter what, unless there is a home-based business involved...

Never let an IRS auditor into your home unless they have a subpoena.

They can, by regulation, visit a business, so if your business is in the home or if you take a home office deduction, they can visit that site. I try to get them to look at pictures or I make them look through a window. If the business is being audited who has an out of the home office, you have to let them visit. However, the auditor can be restricted to public areas only.

4. Random Audits

IRS agents aren't looking for anything in particular when they send out random audit requests to a sample of random taxpayer to review their return. They may review one part of a return or the IRS, may want to review the entire return, line by line. Let's hope this never happens to you.

There are three major ways you are chosen for a random audit: if the return looks wrong (for example, taking too many deductions in comparison to income), randomly chosen ("luck of the draw"), or via Discriminant Function System (DIF) score. This is a *super-secret* scoring of your return. The criteria are unknown to the public, but if your DIF score indicates it, then you will get an audit notice.

Avoiding an Audit

First, do not be afraid to take all the deductions you are allowed to take as long as you can document them. Documentation is key to reducing the risk for an audit (other than a random audit, which, again, is the bad luck of the draw). You need to have your receipts, logs, calendars, forms and other proof of payment. There is no secret formula based on number of deductions taken. There is no "allowed amount". You have to prove all of your deductions.

When there is anything questionable or unusual on your tax return, you need not wait for the IRS to audit. Simply include the explanation (disclosure statement) with your return. Provide enough detail that if the IRS wants to question you, they know the extent of the issue. Yes, this probably means filing the tax return on paper and not electronically.

You may also voluntarily disclose something on the return. Why would you want to do that? Does it not bring the position or the item to the IRS' attention and that means an audit? Not necessarily. In fact, it may stop an audit in its tracks. Here's an example:

John sold some stock he got as a gift from Mom, but there are some issues.

- Mom bought the stock in 1975.

- Mom doesn't have the records with the purchase price, date, or stock splits or dividend reinvestments, and so on.

John needs to establish some kind of tax basis in order to report the sale on his tax return.

- John does some research and prints out the reports he finds.

- Using that research, John makes his best estimate of the tax basis of the stock.

- John includes a disclosure statement with the tax return explaining the problem with the valuation and his solution.

- John keeps copies of the printouts with his tax files.

There are two major benefits resulting from the use of disclosure statements:

1) If the IRS pulls your tax return for audit, reading your explanation and seeing adequate details might be enough to avoid any further audit.

2) Normally, IRS has three years to audit your tax return after you file it.

   a. However, if you make a substantial (25% or more) understatement of income (or overstatement of expenses), they have six years.

   b. When you provide a detailed disclosure statement, even if you have erred by over 25%, the IRS's audit window is limited to three years instead of six!

Does this mean your disclosure statement will definitely be accepted? Who knows! It may depend on who is reading the return. The IRS may just ask some questions (that is, perform a correspondence audit) or outright deny it. Then, you can appeal—but that issue is beyond the scope of this book.

Preparing Your Return With Audits In Mind

Sometimes, you simply can't avoid an audit. Prepare your tax return with that in mind. Use these tips to makes sure all your bases are covered.

1) Keep copies of all documents that back up your income and expense information in your tax file for the year. That includes the following:

    a. W-2s, 1099s, 1098s, K-1s, *etc.*

    b. Copies of receipts for all major asset purchases ($500 or more)

    c. Copies of all donation receipts

    d. Details about any dependents (proof of age and residence)

    e. Copies of all tax payments (local, state, federal)

    f. Copies of the basis of all assets sold

    g. Copies of accounting records for all businesses

    h. Photos of a home office and schematic of the area

    i. Anything else necessary to support the details you reported on your tax return

2) Review your total itemized deductions.

a. If they are high enough to wipe out your income:

- Consider reducing the expenses that don't carry over.

- Consider using the standard deduction.

b. Determine whether something that is causing you to owe alternative minimum taxes (AMT). In 1982, Congress decided to require taxpayers whose income exceeded a certain amount to add back certain items—or, in other words, disallow the deduction. These items include some medical expenses, state and local income taxes, personal exemptions, and even some mortgage interest.

If you are subject to the AMT, consider:

- Can you move that expense (legally) to another part of your tax return, such as Schedule C, Schedule E, or Schedule F?

- Can you eliminate that expense without increasing your taxes?

With AMT, I refer to this as "Congress Giveth, then Congress Taketh Away."

3) Review your overall net income.

   a. Is it too low to live on, especially considering your family size and the area where you live?

   b. The IRS is looking for unreported income.

c. Include a disclosure statement explaining to the IRS what you lived on—savings, credit cards, loans, *etc.*

4) If there are disputed dependents involved, which is a *very* common problem, take the following steps. When you know that you and your ex-spouse are both going to try to claim the same dependent, defend yourself in advance.

   a. Get a release from your ex-spouse. This is called Form 8332.

   b. If you can't get a release, file your tax return on paper, and include the following:

      • Copy of the part of your divorce agreement that states you are entitled to the dependent.

      • Proof that your child or children lived with you more than half the year, or that your home was the child or children's primary residence (school papers, medical records, *etc.*).

      • A support worksheet showing that you paid more than half the support for your child or children.

      • In recent years, the courts have ruled on the side of the IRS that getting Form 8332 is an absolute necessity. In its absence, you will most likely have to go back to family or civil court for damages.

5) Home offices are also a big audit red flag due to abuse. In the past, you could deduct a home office as a percentage of the square footage of the room divided by the total square footage multiplied by the total of allowed expenses.

Now, there is a safe harbor where you take the square footage of the room (maximum of 300 square feet) multiplied by $5. Use of an experienced tax professional can greatly help you to determine what is an allowable home office. Just having a desk and a computer in a room does not make it a home office.

6) Meals and entertainment are always abused, both by employees and by the self-employed.

Don't be greedy.
Only deduct legitimate business expenses—not
"OK, we said the word 'business', so this is a
business lunch!"

Keep logs of…
dates,
times,
names of companions,
and the business purpose of the meal.

Credit card statements may not be enough. Keep the receipts.

Hopefully, the strategies in this chapter will prevent an audit. If you do get audited, it is best to get representation and let a professional navigate for you.

Do not go it alone.

An IRS notice is a letter you want to read and read carefully.

The best steps to take to having a meaningful but short lived relationship with the IRS where no one gets hurt is to get a tax professional to read that letter.

Chapter 6

Getting a love letter from the Internal Revenue Service

Reading and interpreting an IRS Tax Notice

You received an envelope from the Internal Revenue Service. If it came by regular mail, then you have some time to act on the notice. This does not mean weeks or months—sometimes, it can be as little as 10 days. Many times, a client comes into a professional's office and says that they have a tax problem.

The first question an EA, CPA, or attorney asks is whether the client received any notices. Out comes the bag of unopened notices.

Ignoring a tax notice is not the right approach.

If you received an envelope from your utility or cell phone provider, would you ignore it for months at a time? The same should hold true with a letter from Internal Revenue. There are inefficiencies at the IRS, as in all government agencies; however, the IRS does not send you a notice without a good reason. We also need to recognize that the IRS is not infallible. They do make mistakes. So the sooner the notice is addressed if it was sent in error, the better it is for you.

The IRS also sends out notices via certified mail. Those notices are more serious.

Steps to Take after Getting a Notice or Letter from the IRS

Determine why the IRS contacted you in the first place. The IRS sends notices and letters for the following reasons:

a) You have a balance due (one of the two most common notices).

b) The IRS has changed your return (one of the two most common notices).

c) The IRS wants to make a change to the refund expected, either an increase or a decrease.

d) The IRS has a question about the tax return.

e) The IRS needs to verify your identity.

f) The IRS needs additional information in order to process the return (*i.e.*, you have a missing form).

g) The IRS needs to notify you of delays in processing your return.

The notice may be about a specific issue on your federal tax return or account; or may tell you about changes to your account, ask you for more information, or request a payment.

You can handle most of this correspondence without calling or visiting an IRS office if you follow the instructions in the document. However, like preparing your own tax return, dealing with the IRS can be hazardous to your tax health.

The IRS does not work for the taxpayer, but for the federal government.

They will help you understand the notice, but unless you know the rules of the game, it may be in your best interest to speak with a tax professional who is experienced in these matters.

Remember that if you prepared this return by yourself and you want to use professional help, the professional has to be an EA, CPA, or attorney. If you used an un-enrolled preparer, they can help on a standard notice (such as changes and audits, to name two); however, if the notice is a collection notice (usually sent by certified mail), then they cannot help you.

The worst thing to do when you receive a notice from the IRS is to panic.

Before you proceed, check where the notice came from. The first thing to do is to check the return address to be sure it's from the IRS and not another agency.

If the letter is from the IRS:

The notice will have instructions on how to respond. If you want more details about your tax account, you can order a transcript.

If the letter is from another agency:

Such as a state tax department, you'll need to call that office for an explanation.

If the letter is from the Department of the Treasury Bureau of the Fiscal Service:

These notices are often sent when the IRS takes (offsets) some or part of your tax refund to cover another, non-IRS debt (such as federally backed student loans). The Bureau of the Fiscal Service only facilitates the transfers; it won't have information about your IRS account or where the money is being sent.

Understanding Your Notice

IRS notices and letters are numbered and provide contact information for questions. Both the number and contact information are usually in the upper right corner of the notice. If you can't find the number, or have lost your notice, there are general numbers you can call. The appendix of this book has a list of these notices.

Each notice normally tells you:

- What the IRS is changing on your return or account, or needs more information about.

- Why the IRS is making a change or needs that information.

- Where to send your reply (if a reply is needed) and by when.

There are a few main categories for notices.

Informational Notices

Claiming certain tax credits and other interactions with the IRS may lead the IRS to send you a notice. Most of the time, they are just for your records, and you don't need to reply.

Notices About Changes to Your Tax Return or Account

The IRS may have already made a change, or may be looking at your return to see if there was a mistake. The notice will have instructions on if or how you need to reply.

Some common notices of a change include the following:

- An <u>incorrect return</u>, where you made a mistake.

- <u>Underreporting income</u>, where it's possible you didn't report all your income.

- Notice that you are <u>being audited</u> or the IRS has already audited you and is proposing changes.

Notices Where the IRS Says You Owe Taxes

If you have a balance on your tax account, you'll get a notice letting you know how much you owe, when it's due, and how to pay.

If you can't pay the full amount by that date, you need to figure out what payment options might work for your situation, and act to set up a payment plan or other way to pay off your balance.

Now what If I Want to Talk to Someone about the Notice?

Each notice should include contact information.

Some phone numbers on letters or notices are general IRS toll-free numbers, but if a specific employee is working your case, it will show a specific phone number to reach that employee or the department manager.

Now what If You've Lost Your Notice?

If you've lost your notice, call one of the following toll-free numbers for help:

- Individual taxpayers: 800-829-1040 (TTY/TDD 1-800-829-4059)
- Business taxpayers: 800-829-4933

Understanding Specific Notices and Letters

All notices and letters are identified by a code, usually shown in the upper right corner of page 1 of the notice. If it is a letter, the identifier may be in the bottom left. The most common of these are identified by a two-letter code called a CP (short for Computer Paragraph). The number associated with the notice, such as CP2000, means "Computer Paragraph 2000."

Here are the most common and most important notices and letters with the best direction to take.

Now what?
I got a CP2000 Notice from the IRS.
Help!

If you receive a CP2000 notice, it indicates that the income and/or payment information that the IRS has on file doesn't match the information reported on the tax return. This could affect the tax return by causing an increase or decrease in the tax. It also may not change the return at all.

It is not a bill for taxes due, although it does look like one...

If the IRS says there is something different between what they have and what you reported on the return, they will presume that what they have is correct, and the notice will show what was reported versus what they have on file. The IRS will compute a new tax and give you the option of either paying the discrepancy in full or disputing some or all of their findings.

The Service gets their information from forms filed with the agency, such as W2s, 1099s, and so on. One of the most common reasons for receiving a CP2000 is omitting an amount from a 1099, whether it is interest of dividends. It is at times like this that it is simple to reconcile the notice to the return. If the IRS is correct, pay the tax (and interest and penalties, if included) and you are done.

A more complicated situation arises if you did not report the sales of certain investments. For example, your financial advisor sold 40 different stock holdings. The financial services company sends you a 1099B with a detailed accounting of all 40 transactions and sends the IRS the 1099B, which lists just the sales date and sales price (especially if the purchase of the investment was before 2011).

As you prepared your return, you inadvertently omitted 5, thus reporting only 35. The IRS computers will initiate the CP2000, telling you that they are missing some of the sales details. Generally, the IRS will include the sales price of the investment and not give you the benefit of your basis or cost. This overstates the gain, and in some cases, you may have a loss. This is just one of the situations where a tax professional will be able to help you navigate the process.

This book previously mentions penalties and interest. If you do owe tax, the IRS will assess interest on the balance due, and it is rare that the interest will be removed. When penalties are added ("assessed"), you do have options for having those removed. The penalty will be for late paying the additional tax, and is usually assessed at 0.5% per month.

Depending on the amount of tax, the penalty amount can be large or small, and again depending on the amount, there are mechanisms for having the penalty removed or abated. An experienced tax professional will be helpful to explain the process. A sample CP2000 notice is in the next page.

Department of Treasury
Internal Revenue Service
AUR CORR 5-E08-113
PHILADELPHIA PA 19255-0521

012345.678901.2345.678 2 AT 0.345 1234

FIRST M & FIRST M LAST
STREET ADDRESS
CHAMPIONS GT FL 33896-9613

xxxxxx

Notice	CP2000
Tax Year	2011
Notice date	May 29, 2013
Social Security number	XXX-XX-XXXX
AUR control number	XXXXXXXX
To contact us	Phone 1-800-829-8310 Fax 1-877-477-0602
Page 1 of 8	

XXXXXXXXXXXXXX

Proposed changes to your 2011 Form 1040
Amount due: $320

The income and payment information we have on file from sources such as employers or financial institutions doesn't match the information you reported on your tax return. If our information is correct, you will owe $320 (including interest), which you need to pay by June 27, 2013.

Summary of proposed changes

Tax you owe	$309
Payments	$0
Interest	$11
Amount due by June 27, 2013	**$320**

What you need to do immediately

Review this notice, and compare our changes to the information on your 2011 tax return.

If you agree with the changes we made
* Complete, sign and date the Response form on Page 5, and mail it to us along with your payment of $320 so we receive it by June 27, 2013.
* If you can't pay the amount due, pay as much as you can now, and make payment arrangements that allow you to payoff the rest over time. If you want to apply for an installment plan, send in your Response form AND a completed Installment Agreement Request (Form 9465). Download Form 9465 from www.irs.gov, or call 1-800-829-3676 to request a copy. You can also save time and money by applying online if you qualify. Visit www.irs.gov, and search for keyword: "tax payment options" for more information about:
  — Installment and payment agreements
  — Payroll deductions
  — Credit card payments

If you don't agree with the changes
Complete the Response form on Page 5, and send it to us along with a signed statement and any documentation that supports your claim so we receive it by June 27, 2013.

If we don't hear from you

If we don't receive your response by June 27, 2013, we will send you a Statutory Notice of Deficiency followed by a final bill for the proposed amount due. During this time, interest will increase and penalties may apply.

Continued on back...

Now what?
I got a CP71 (A–D) Notice from the IRS. Help!

The 71C, which I call the "annual birthday card," is the most common of Notices 71A–D. It is an annual notice that the IRS sends out reminding the taxpayer of the amount that is still owed, including the assessment of additional interest and penalties. Taxpayers will get these notices even if they are on an installment plan.

These are nothing to worry about as far as levies or liens are concerned.

They should be checked and kept in your file to make sure that they are correct and that nothing else was added to the amount indicated on the prior year's notice. A sample CP71C notice is in the next page.

Department of Treasury
Internal Revenue Service

Notice	CP71C
Tax year	
Notice date	February 9, 2016
Social Security number	
To contact us	Phone
Your caller ID	
Page 1 of 3	

Annual reminder of balance due taxes for tax year [2013]

Amount due:

The law requires us to send you this annual reminder notice explaining the amount you still owe for your ___ Form ___ taxes.

If you are already working with us to address the amount you owe, you don't need to do anything. However, if you have questions about this notice, you should ask your IRS representative.

To prevent interest and penalties from continuing to increase, pay the amount due by [February 19, 2016].

Billing Summary

Amount you owe	
Interest charges	
Amount due by February 19, 2016	

What you need to do immediately

If you agree with the amount due and you're not working with an IRS representative

• Pay the amount due of ___ by [February 19, 2016], to prevent interest from continuing to increase.
• Send us a check or money order with the payment stub or use one of the other payment options in this notice.

Continued on back....

IRS

Notice	CP71C
Notice date	February 9, 2016
Social security number	

Payment

• Make your check or money order payable to the United States Treasury.
• Write your social security number, the tax year ___, and the form number ___ on your payment and any correspondence.

INTERNAL REVENUE SERVICE

Amount due by
February 19, 2016

Now What?
I got a CP21C Notice from the IRS.
Help!

You will get this notice when you request a change to be made to your tax return via, for example, an amended return. If the change results in an expected refund or a tax due, which you paid, you will see a notice that shows a zero balance. A sample CP21C is shown below.

Department of the Treasury
Internal Revenue Service
Stop 6525 (SC CIS),
Kansas City MO 64999-0025

Notice	CP21C
Tax Year	2016
Notice date	June 12, 2017
Social Security number	
To contact us	1-800-829-8374
Page 1 of 1	CAF 29H

26004

Changes to your 2016 Form 1040

Amount due: $0.00

We made the changes you requested to your 2016 Form 1040 to adjust your Schedule E income (or loss).

As a result you don't owe us any money, nor are you due a refund.

Summary

Account balance before this change	$ -631.00
Increase in tax	631.00
Amount due	**$0.00**

What you need to do

If you agree with the changes we made
• You don't need to respond to this notice.

If you don't agree with the changes
Call 1-800-829-8374 to review your account with a representative. Be sure you have your account information available when you call.

We'll assume you agree with the information in this notice if we don't hear from you.

Additional information

• Visit www.irs.gov/cp21c
• For tax forms, instructions, and publications, visit www.irs.gov or call 1-800-TAX-FORM (1-800-829-3676).
• You can contact us by mail at the address at the top of this notice. Be sure to include your social security number, the tax year, and the form number you are writing about.
• Keep this notice for your records.

We're required to send a copy of this notice to both you and your spouse. Each copy contains the information you are authorized to receive.
If you need assistance, please don't hesitate to contact us.

Now what?
I got a CP14H Notice from the IRS.
Help!

This is one of the more recent notices that the IRS issues. If your tax return shows that a portion of your overall tax liability has to do with the shared responsibility payment, this notice is generated. It is not a change notice, but one that is for the taxpayer's information.

As of the writing of this book, the individual shared responsibility provision of the Affordable Care Act requires you and each member of your family to have qualifying health care coverage (called minimum essential coverage), qualify for a coverage exemption, or make an individual shared responsibility payment when you file your income tax return.

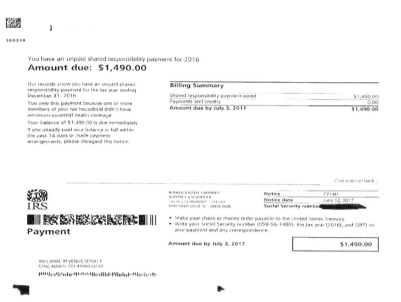

Now What?
I got a CP10 Notice from the IRS.
Help!

Receiving a CP10 means the IRS has adjusted your tax return, which affected the amount of the refund applied to the following year's estimated tax payments, as requested on the tax return.

The notice explains the changes to the tax return and the resulting adjustment to the amount applied to the estimated payments. You should adjust your tax return and estimated payment records to match the IRS records if you agree with the change. A sample CP10 notice can be seen below.

Now what?
I got a CP16 Notice from the IRS.
Help!

A CP16 notice means that the IRS has adjusted your tax return, and these changes have affected your refund. The notice explains the changes to the tax return and the amount of the overpayment that was applied to your tax balance from prior year returns.

If you agree with the adjustment, make the changes to your tax return records to reflect the IRS adjustment. If you do not agree with the change, call or write to the IRS at the phone number or address given in the header section of the notice. A sample CP16 notice can be seen below.

Now What?
I got a CP49 Notice from the IRS.
Help!

This notice informs the taxpayer that the IRS is taking all or a portion of the overpayment (that is, a refund) from one account and applying it to an underpayment (that is, a balance due) for another account. There may be additional information on the notice regarding protection from your spouse's debts (this is called Injured Spouse Relief). A sample CP49 notice is shown below.

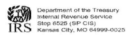

Department of the Treasury	
Internal Revenue Service	
Stop 6525 (SP CIS)	
Kansas City, MO 64999-0025	

Notice	CP49
Tax year	2016
Notice date	January 30, 2017
Social security number	nnn-nn-nnnn
To contact us	Phone 1-800-829-0922
Your caller ID	nnnn
Page 1 of 2	

s018999546711s
JOHN AND MARY SMITH
123 N HARRIS ST
HARVARD, TX 12345

We applied your 2016 Form 1040 overpayment to an unpaid balance

Refund due: $250.00

We applied $500.00 of your 2016 Form 1040 overpayment to an amount owed for 2015.

As a result, your refund has been reduced to $250.00.

Summary

Overpayment for 2016	$500.00
Amount applied to tax owed for 2015	-250.00
Remaining balance for 2015	0.00
Refund due	**$250.00**

What you need to do

Your refund

- If you haven't already received a refund check for $250.00, you should receive it within 2-3 weeks as long as you don't owe other tax or debt we're required to collect.
- Since additional processing was required to correct your tax account, we were unable to deposit your refund directly to your bank account as you requested. We are issuing your refund by check.

Protection from your spouse's debt

When you file a joint tax return, you may be able to prevent some or all of your overpayment from paying liabilities for which your spouse (or former spouse) is responsible. For example, if some or all of your overpayment from a joint return has been (or will be) applied to pay your spouse's past-due income taxes, health coverage shared responsibility payment, or other debt (child support, spousal support, student loans), you may be entitled to relief as an injured spouse. If you're eligible, you may be entitled to a refund for your share of an overpayment that's been (or will be) applied to your spouse's debt. For more information, or to submit a claim, go to www.irs.gov and download the Injured Spouse Allocation (Form 8379) or call 1-800-829-3676 to request a copy.

Now what?
I got a CP59 Notice from the IRS.
Help!

If you have received this notice, it means you have failed to file a tax return. The type of return you failed to file and the relevant tax period will be shown in the upper right corner of the notice, as well as in the body of the notice. You received this notice because the IRS has reason to think you meet the filing requirements and they have not received a return.

You will either need to file your return as soon as possible or explain to the IRS why you don't need to file via letter or phone call. Your EA, CPA, or attorney would be the best option to help you communicate this to the IRS. A sample CP59 notice is shown below.

IRS
Department of Treasury
Internal Revenue Service
[   ]

Notice	CP59
Tax Year	[XXXX]
Notice Date	October 10, 2016
Social Security number	
To contact us	Phone 1-800-
Your Caller ID:	
Select code	
Page 1 of 4	

Message about your 2010 Form 1040
You didn't file a Form 1040 tax return

Our records show that you haven't filed your tax return for the tax year ending on December 31, 2010.

What you need to do immediately
If you are required to file a tax return for 2010, please do so immediately.
- Complete and sign all required tax forms, include a payment for any taxes due, and mail us your return using the envelope provided.
- If you can't pay the amount due, pay as much as you can now and make payment arrangements that allow you to pay off the rest over time. Visit www.irs.gov and search for keyword "tax payment options" for more information about:
  - Installment and payment agreements—download required forms or save time and money by applying online using the Online Payment Agreement application if you qualify
  - Automatic payment deductions from your bank account
  - Payroll deductions
  - Credit card payments
  - Or, call us at 1-800-   to discuss your options.
- You risk losing your refund if you don't file your return. If you are due a refund for withholding or estimated taxes, you must file your return to claim it by [return due date + 3 years + any extension of time to file]. The same rule applies to a right to claim tax credits such as the Earned Income Credit.
- **Or if you don't think you had to file a tax return for 2010.** Complete the Response form on Page 3 to indicate whether any of the circumstances below apply to you. Send us the form in the enclosed envelope.
Indicate whether:
- You already filed a tax return for 2010 (if so, send us a signed and dated copy of the return along with your Response form).
- The person addressed on this notice is deceased and you already filed a Form 1041, Income Tax Return for Estates and Trusts.
- You don't think you are required to file for one of the reasons listed on Page 3.

If we don't hear from you
- If you don't file a tax return, or dispute this notice if you feel you've received it in error, we may determine your tax for you.
- You may continue to accrue penalties and interest charges on the amount of tax due.

Now what?
I got a CP90 Notice from the IRS.
Help!

This notice notifies you of your unpaid taxes and that the IRS intends to levy or legally seize property to collect the amount owed. This notice and referenced publications explain how to request an appeal if you do not agree. You need to file a Form 12153, Request for A Collection Due Process Hearing, and send it to the address shown on your levy notice within 30 days from the date of the letter in order to appeal the action with the Office of Appeals.

You should pay the balance due, or if the full payment cannot be made at this time, contact the IRS immediately at the number listed on the notice. The notice gives you 30 days from the date of the notice to pay the debt, to enter into an installment agreement, or to propose an offer in compromise (see chapter 7). You also have the right to file a request for an Appeals Collection Due Process (CDP) hearing request as described in Publication 1660, which is usually enclosed with the notice.

If you don't pay, or make arrangements to pay the balance due, the IRS may levy against any federal payments due to you.

They may also file a Federal Tax Lien giving them legal claim to your property as security or payment for your tax debt. A sample CP90 is shown below.

Notice Number:
Notice Date: DEC. 31, 2012
Social Security Number:

Collection Assistance:
1-800-829-3903
(Asistencia en español disponible)
Caller ID:

Final Notice
Notice Of Intent To Levy And Notice Of Your Right To A Hearing
PLEASE RESPOND IMMEDIATELY

We previously asked you to pay the federal tax shown on the next page, but we haven't received your payment. This letter is your notice of our intent to levy under Internal Revenue Code (IRC) Section 6331 and your right to appeal under IRC Section 6330.

We may also file a Notice of Federal Tax Lien at any time to protect the government's interest. A lien is a public notice to your creditors that the government has a right to your current assets, including any assets you acquire after we file the lien.

If you don't pay the amount you owe, make alternative arrangements to pay, or request an appeals hearing within 30 days from the date of this letter, we may take your property, or rights to property. Property includes real estate, automobiles, business assets, bank accounts, wages, commissions, social security benefits, and other income. We've enclosed Publication 594, which has more information about our collection process; Publication 1660, which explains your appeal rights; and Form 12153, which you can use to request a Collection Due Process hearing with our Appeals Office. To preserve your right to contest Appeals' decision in the U.S. Tax Court, you must complete, sign, and return Form 12153 within 30 days from the date of this letter.

To prevent collection action, please send your full payment today.

- Make your check or money order payable to United States Treasury.
- Write your Social Security Number on your payment.
- Send your payment and the attached payment voucher to us in the enclosed envelope. The amount you owe is shown on the next page.

90

Now what?
I got a CP501 Notice from the IRS.
Help!

This is the first reminder notice that you have a balance due on a tax account. The IRS has previously sent a notice about a balance due on a tax account. This reminder notice alerts you that there is an outstanding balance, and, if the balance is not paid within 21 days, the possible actions the IRS may take. A sample CP501 notice is shown below.

Department of the Treasury
Internal Revenue Service
Holtsville, NY 11742-0480

Notice	CP501
Tax year	2016
Notice date	January 30, 2017
Social security number	NNN-NN-NNNN
To contact us	1-800-829-0922
Your caller ID	NNNN
Page 1 of 6	

s018999546711s

JAMES & KAREN Q. HINDS
22 BOULDER STREET
HANSON, CT 00000-7253

You have unpaid taxes for 2016

Amount due: $9,533.53

Our records show you have unpaid
taxes for the tax year ended December
31, 2016 (Form 1040NR).

If you already paid your balance in full
within the last 21 days or made
payment arrangements, please
disregard this notice.

If you already have an installment or
payment agreement in place for this
tax year, then continue with that
agreement

Billing Summary

Amount you owed	$9,444.07
Failure-to-pay penalty	34.98
Interest charges	54.48
Amount due by February 20, 2017	**$9,533.53**

**If you are a debtor in a bankruptcy case, this notice is for your
information only and is not intended to seek payment outside of the
bankruptcy process of taxes due before you filed your petition. You
will not receive another notice of the balance due while the
automatic stay remains in effect.**

Continued on back...

James Q. Hinds
22 Boulder Street
Hanson, CT 00000-7253

Notice	CP501
Notice date	January 30, 2017
Social security number	NNN-NN-NNNN

Payment

- Make your check or money order payable to the United States Treasury.
- Write your social security number (NNN-NN-NNNN), the tax year (2016), and form number (1040NR) on your payment.

INTERNAL REVENUE SERVICE
CINCINNATI, OH 45999-0149
s018999546711s

- **Amount due by**
  February 20, 2017

$9,533.53

Now what?
I got a CP523 Notice from the IRS.
Help!

This is the notice you receive if you have an installment agreement with the IRS for an outstanding tax balance and the IRS considers you to be in default on the installment agreement. Examples of default causing actions include missing a payment, having a new balance due, or not filing a tax return. The notice also informs you of what the IRS intends to do to collect the taxes owed, which can include filing a federal tax lien or seizing (levying) your wages and/or bank accounts.

Call the IRS at the phone number listed in the header section to determine what steps to take to correct the problem. You have 30 days from the date of the notice to contact the IRS and resolve the issue.

If you don't agree with the reason for the cancellation of the installment agreement, call the number at the top of the notice to discuss it with the IRS. The installment agreement may be reinstated (an additional fee may apply), or if the issue cannot be resolved, you have the right to file an appeal. A sample CP523 notice is shown below.

Department of the Treasury
Internal Revenue Service
Austin, TX 73301-0030

Notice	CP523
Tax period	2014
Notice date	January 30, 2017
Social security number	NNN-NN-NNNN
To contact us	1-800-829-0922
Your caller ID	NNNN
Page 1 of 6	

s018999546711s
JAMES & KAREN Q. HINDS
22 BOULDER STREET
HANSON, CT 00000-7253

Notice of intent to levy

Intent to terminate your installment agreement
Amount due immediately: $600.00

The monthly payment for your installment agreement is overdue. Because we didn't receive one or more payments from you, as your installment agreement requires, you have until March 3, 2017, to make a payment or we will terminate your installment agreement.

In addition, this notice is your notice of intent to levy. We can seize (levy) any state tax refund you're entitled to and apply it to your $10,803.20 in overdue taxes on or after May 2, 2017.

Billing Summary

Amount you owed	$9,444.07
Failure-to-pay penalty	34.98
Interest charges	1,324.15
Amount due immediately	**$600.00**

Continued on back...

IRS

James Q. Hinds
22 Boulder Street
Hanson, CT 00000-7253

Notice	CP523
Notice date	January 30, 2017
Social Security number	NNN-NN-NNNN

Payment

- Make your check or money order payable to the United States Treasury.
- Write your social security number (NNN-NN-NNNN), the tax year (2014), and form number (1040) on your payment.

INTERNAL REVENUE SERVICE
AUSTIN, TX 73301-0030
s018999546711s

- **Amount due immediately**

	$600.00

‖‖‖ ‖‖‖‖‖ ‖‖‖‖‖‖‖ ‖‖‖‖‖‖ ‖‖‖

Now what?
I got a CP504 Notice from the IRS.
Help!

If you are receiving this notice, the IRS has previously sent notices about a balance due on a tax account; this is **THE** final notice. This urgent notice alerts you that there is an outstanding balance, and the IRS intends to levy or take your state tax refund to pay it. A sample CP504 notice is shown below.

Department of the Treasury
Internal Revenue Service
Holtsville, NY 11742-0480

Notice	CP504
Tax year	2016
Notice date	January 30, 2017
Social security number	NNN-NN-NNNN
To contact us	1-800-829-0922
Your caller ID	NNNN
Page 1 of 6	

s018999546711s
JAMES & KAREN Q. HINDS
22 BOULDER STREET
HANSON, CT 00000-7253

Notice of intent to seize (levy) your property or rights to property
Amount due immediately: $9,533.53

This is a notice of intent to levy your state tax refund or other property. As we notified you before, our records show you have unpaid taxes for the tax year ended December 31, 2016 (Form 1040A). If you don't call us immediately to make payment arrangements or pay the amount due, we may levy your property or rights to property and apply it to the $9,533.53 you owe.

Billing Summary

Amount you owed	$9,444.07
Failure-to-pay penalty	34.98
Interest charges	54.48
Amount due immediately	**$9,533.53**

What you need to do immediately

If you agree with the amount due and you're not working with an IRS representative

- Pay the amount due of $9,533.53 immediately or we may file Notice of Federal Tax Lien, the amount of interest will increase, and additional penalties may apply.
- Pay online or mail a check or money order with the attached payment stub. **You can pay online now at www.irs.gov/payments.**

Continued on back...

James Q. Hinds
22 Boulder Street
Hanson, CT 00000-7253

Payment

Notice	CP504
Notice date	January 30, 2017
Social security number	NNN-NN-NNNN

- Make your check or money order payable to the United States Treasury.
- Write your social security number (NNN-NN-NNNN), the tax year (2016), and form number (1040A) on your payment.

INTERNAL REVENUE SERVICE
CINCINNATI, OH 45999-0149
s018999546711s

- **Pay immediately**

$9,533.53

Now what?
I got a Letter 11, Final Notice of Intent to Levy and Notice of Your Right to a Hearing from the IRS.
Help!

This letter is to notify you of unpaid taxes, and inform you that the Service intends to levy to collect the amount owed. The letter and referenced publications explain how to request an appeal if you do not agree.

You need to file a Form 12153, *Request for A Collection Due Process Hearing*, and send it to the address shown on your levy notice within 30 days from the date of the letter in order to appeal the proposed action with the Office of Appeals.

Now What?
I got a Letter 525, General 30 Day Letter from the IRS.
Help!

You receive this letter with a computation report of proposed adjustments to your tax return. It outlines your options if you do not agree with the proposed adjustments. If you agree with the adjustment, you sign and return the agreement form. If you do not agree, you can submit a request for appeal to the office or individual that sent you the letter.

The letter contains information on filing an appeal or protest, and lists IRS publications on how to file. You need to file your protest within 30 days from the date on this letter in order to appeal the proposed adjustments with the Office of Appeals.

Now What?
I got a Letter 531, Notice of Deficiency from the IRS.
Help!

You will get this letter if you owe additional tax or other assessed amounts (*i.e.*, interest and penalties) for the tax year(s) listed in the letter. The letter explains how to dispute the adjustments if you do not agree. If you want to dispute the adjustments without payment, you will have 90 days from the notice date to file a petition with the Tax Court.

Now what?
I got a Letter 692, Request for Consideration of Additional Findings from the IRS.
Help!

You receive this letter with a computation report of proposed adjustments to your tax return. It outlines your options if you do not agree with the proposed adjustments. If you agree with the adjustment, you sign and return the agreement form. If you do not agree, you can submit a request for appeal to the office or individual that sent you the letter. The letter contains information on filing an appeal or protest, and lists IRS publications on how to file. You need to file your protest within 15 days from the date on this letter in order to appeal the proposed adjustments with the Office of Appeals.

Now what?
I got a Letter 950, 30 Day Letter-Straight Deficiency or Over-Assessment from the IRS.
Help!

This letter is used for un-agreed, straight deficiency, straight overassessment or mixed deficiency and overassessment cases. This letter may be used for various types of tax. If you agree with the adjustment, you sign and return the agreement form. If you do not agree, you can submit a request for appeal to the office or individual that sent you the letter.

The letter contains information on filing an appeal or protest, and lists IRS publications on how to file. You need to file your protest within 30 days from the date on this letter in order to appeal the proposed adjustments with the Office of Appeals.

Now what?
I got a Letter 1058, Final Notice Reply within 30 Days from the IRS.
Help!

This letter is a final notice to notify you of unpaid taxes, and inform you that the Service intends to levy to collect the amount owed. The letter and referenced publications explain how to request an appeal if you do not agree. You need to file a Form 12153, Request for A Collection Due Process Hearing, and send it to the address shown on your levy notice within 30 days from the date of the letter in order to appeal the action with the Office of Appeals.

Top 10 Most Uncommon Common Forms

1. Form 5329 – Compute the penalty on an early distribution of an IRA or other retirement plan

2. Schedule E – which part I (Rental Property) or II (S-corp, partnership or other pass-through items)

3. Schedule H – Compute the tax on your household help (maid, butler, nanny)

4. Schedule F – profit and loss related to farming

5. Form 2555 – Foreign Income Exclusion

6. Form 3115 – Change in Accounting Method or Period

7. Form 2210 – Penalty for Underpayment of Estimated Tax

8. Form 4684 – Reporting your Casualty or Theft Loss

9. Form 433 (et al) – Financial Statement for Installment Agreement or Offer in Compromise

10. Form 3520 – Reporting Assets in a Foreign Owned Trust

If you didn't locate your notice in this section, it may be a less common one.

The IRS has many more notices, and the less common ones are listed in the appendix.

All hands on deck.

The moment you pull an IRS Notice from your mailbox, you need to open it and call an enrolled agent immediately.

Chapter 7

You got a tax notice.
You cannot run or hide, so now what?

What to do when the IRS wants something from you.

Say you are in a situation where the IRS has requested an action or documentation from you. As previously mentioned, a tax professional will be able to guide you through this process and place you in the best possible light. But, if you want to handle it by yourself, it is best to give the IRS exactly what they ask, nothing more.

Never provide voluntary information or documentation.

A common situation involves a tax due, possibly with penalties and interest assessed. If you cannot pay the tax, there are options available to most taxpayers.

IRS Fresh Start Program

The IRS Fresh Start program makes it easier for taxpayers and even small businesses to pay back taxes and avoid tax liens. Here are three important features of the Fresh Start program:

- **Tax Liens**

    The Fresh Start program increased the amount that taxpayers can owe before the IRS generally will file a Notice of Federal Tax Lien. That amount is now $10,000; however, in some cases, the IRS may still file a lien notice on amounts less than $10,000.

    When a taxpayer meets certain requirements and pays off their tax debt, the IRS may now withdraw a filed Notice of Federal Tax Lien. Taxpayers must request this in writing using Form 12277, Application for Withdrawal.

    Some taxpayers may qualify to have their lien notice withdrawn if they are paying their tax debt through a Direct Debit installment agreement. Taxpayers also need to request this in writing by using Form 12277.

    If a taxpayer defaults on the Direct Debit Installment Agreement, the IRS may file a new Notice of Federal Tax Lien and resume collection actions.

- **Installment Agreements.**

    The Fresh Start program expanded access to streamlined installment agreements. Now, individual taxpayers who owe up to $50,000 can pay through monthly direct debit payments for up to 72 months (six years). While the IRS generally will not need a financial statement, they may need some financial information from the taxpayer. The easiest way to apply for a payment plan is to use the Online Payment Agreement tool at IRS.gov. If you don't have Web access, you may file Form 9465, Installment Agreement, to apply.

Taxpayers in need of installment agreements for tax debts more than $50,000 or longer than six years still need to provide the IRS with a financial statement. In these cases, the IRS may ask for one of two forms: either Collection Information Statement, Form 433-A; or Form 433-F.

- **Offers in Compromise.**

    An offer in compromise (OIC) is an agreement that allows taxpayers to settle their tax debt for less than the full amount. Fresh Start expanded and streamlined the OIC program. The IRS now has more flexibility when analyzing a taxpayer's ability to pay. This makes the offer program available to a larger group of taxpayers.

    Generally, the IRS will accept an offer if it represents the most the agency can expect to collect within a reasonable period of time. The IRS will not accept an offer if it believes that the taxpayer can pay the amount owed in full as a lump sum or through a payment agreement.

    The IRS looks at several factors, including the taxpayer's income and assets, to make a decision regarding the taxpayer's ability to pay. Use the Offer in Compromise Pre-Qualifier tool on IRS.gov
    (https://irs.treasury.gov/oic_pre_qualifier/) to see if you may be eligible for an OIC.

The Differences between a Tax Lien and a Tax Levy

Tax liens and tax levies are staples of the IRS's tax debt collection enforcement machinery. They are two very common methods the IRS uses to get the money it's owed if a taxpayer doesn't write a check voluntarily, or for that matter, quickly enough.

Tax Liens

A tax lien is a claim on your property as a result of failing to pay tax debt. A lien first arises when a person, who owes tax, fails to pay the tax after an official "demand" by the IRS. The lien is sometimes referred to as a "secret lien" because even though at first there is no public record, it attaches to all of the taxpayer's property and rights to property—both real estate and personal property—as of the date the tax is assessed.

In consequence, if taxes are assessed against you on July 1st and you give property to a third party as a gift on July 2nd, a tax lien continues to be attached to that property, even though you had no knowledge of the existence of the tax lien and even though the person who received the property didn't know that the tax lien had arisen.

This occurs frequently in divorces, when one spouse who owes taxes to the IRS transfers ownership of property to the other spouse as part of a marital dissolution. Even though neither spouse is aware of the tax lien, it continues to be attached to the property now in the hands of the spouse who didn't have any tax liability, and the IRS can collect the taxes owed by seizing and selling the property.

Certain third parties are protected from the impact of the secret tax lien.

These are generally people who gave "fair value" for the property received. For example, if your home was subject to a secret IRS tax lien and you sold it to a third party for its fair market value, the IRS could not seize your home once it had been transferred to someone else. To be clear, this rule would not be of any help if the person who received the home paid less than its actual value.

When most taxpayers or tax professionals refer to a tax lien, they are actually referring to a "Notice of Federal Tax Lien" (NFTL). An NFTL is a document filed in a public place, such as a county recorder's office or with the Secretary of State. It is a notice to the world that you owe taxes. A Notice of Federal Tax Lien generally lists the amount of the taxes owed, the type of tax, and even the years for which taxes are owed. It also lists the date the tax was assessed. It is worth noting that the Notice of Federal Tax Lien is a static document; therefore, if you make payments on your tax liability, the NFTL will continue to list the same amount due. Likewise, as interest and penalties accrue, the document will not be updated to reflect the additional amounts due.

That is why the amount listed in the NFTL is not a true reflection of your tax liabilities.

The Notice of Federal Tax Lien will be picked up by the various credit reporting agencies, and will cause significant credit problems. The tax lien does not, however, take any money out of your bank account. If you own real property and try to sell it, the IRS will be paid the equity in your property.

Tax Levies

A levy is the IRS collecting a debt you owe through the seizure of your property. A tax levy is not available for the general public to see, and does not by itself affect your credit rating or prevent you from selling your property. However, if the IRS serves a tax levy on your bank, then the bank is required to send all your money to the IRS. The bank cannot immediately send your funds to the IRS. Instead, the Internal Revenue Code specifies that the bank must hold onto the funds for 21 calendar days. The bank will notify you of its receipt of the tax levy, but receiving the notification may take until a few days after the bank receives it, and that 21-day clock will continue to tick.

The 21-day holding period is extremely important because it gives you an opportunity to negotiate with the IRS to release the tax levy before the bank sends the funds. While it can be difficult to get the IRS to agree to release the tax levy, an experienced tax litigation attorney can sometimes get this accomplished.

Whether this is possible in a given situation will depend on your overall situation, including such factors as the following:

- How much money you have in the bank.

- The value of your other assets.

- The amount of your income and expenses.

- The total amount of your tax bill.

- Whether you have been cooperating with the IRS by responding to their inquiries.

Don't expect to get rapid notification from the IRS that they have sent a tax levy. The internal operating procedures of the IRS, known as the Internal Revenue Manual, specifically instruct its employees to delay sending a copy of the tax levy to the taxpayer.

A tax levy sent to the bank is a "one shot" tax levy. It only attaches to the funds in your account at the minute a tax levy is received. A tax levy on wages, commissions, or other similar payments also exists, and is called a continuing levy. Under a continuing levy, unless the IRS agrees to release the levy, your employer will continue to send the bulk of your paycheck to the IRS until your entire tax liability has been satisfied.

The amount that can be sent is different for everyone and is based on what they owe and what their gross income. Generally, federal law provides that any garnishment can be no more than 25% of your disposable income, or the amount that your income exceeds 30 times the federal minimum wage, whichever is less. Disposable earnings are defined as that portion of one's income that a person is free to spend or invest as he or she sees fit, after payment of taxes and other obligations.

Legally mandated deductions are those for the payment of taxes and Social Security.

The tax code, however, limits only what the IRS is required to *leave*. The IRS will take as much as it can and leave you with an amount that the tax code says is necessary for you to pay for basic living necessities. The amount that you can keep corresponds to the number of exemptions you claim for tax purposes.

Refer to https://www.irs.gov/pub/irs-pdf/p1494.pdf, which is updated yearly, to see how much of your wages are protected.

For example, a single person getting paid weekly in 2017 and claiming five exemptions will only be allowed to keep $511.54. A married person filing a 2017 joint return, getting paid monthly, and claiming two exemptions will only be allowed to keep $1,733.33. Anything over and above these amounts gets garnished and sent to the IRS. So, if the married person in our example makes $3,000 per month, he will only get to keep $1,733.33, and $1,266.67 will go to the IRS.

If the IRS sends a tax levy to your employer, your employer is required to send the required amount to the IRS and because there is no 21-day holding period, the tax levy is effective starting with the very first paycheck you receive after the employer receives the tax levy. In addition, because there is no holding period, if you find out the IRS has served a tax levy on your employer, it is extremely important to engage a qualified tax professional to begin immediate negotiations with your employer *before* your next paycheck. Remember, once your funds have been forwarded to the IRS, either by the bank or your employer, you are not getting them back.

The IRS may levy (seize) assets such as wages, bank accounts, social security benefits, and retirement income. The IRS may also seize your property (including your car, boat, or real estate) and sell the property to satisfy the tax debt. In addition, any future federal tax refunds or state income tax refunds that you're due may be seized and applied to your federal tax liability.

Understanding a Federal Tax Lien

A federal tax lien is the government's legal claim against your property when you fail to pay a tax debt. The lien protects the government's interest in all your property, including real estate, personal property, and financial assets.

A federal tax lien exists after the IRS takes the following actions:

- Puts your balance due on the books (assesses your liability).

- Sends you a bill that explains how much you owe (Notice and Demand for Payment)

- Then, if you neglect or refuse to fully pay the debt in time...

The IRS files a public document, the Notice of Federal Tax Lien, to alert creditors that the government has a legal right to your property.

How to Get Rid of a Lien

Paying your tax debt in full is the best way to get rid of a federal tax lien. The IRS releases your lien within 30 days after you have paid your tax debt.

When conditions are in the best interest of both the government and the taxpayer, other options for reducing the impact of a lien exist.

Discharge of Property

A "discharge" removes the lien from specific property. There are several Internal Revenue Code (IRC) provisions that determine eligibility.

Subordination

"Subordination" does not remove the lien, but allows other creditors to move ahead of the IRS, which may make it easier to get a loan or mortgage.

Withdrawal

A "withdrawal" removes the public Notice of Federal Tax Lien and assures that the IRS is not competing with other creditors for your property; however, you are still liable for the amount due.

Two additional withdrawal options resulted from the Fresh Start initiative.

Option one may allow withdrawal of your Notice of Federal Tax Lien after the lien's release. General eligibility for this option includes the following:

- Your tax liability has been satisfied and your lien has been released.

- You have been in compliance for the past three years in filing all individual returns, business returns, and information returns.

- You are current on your estimated tax payments and federal tax deposits, as applicable.

  Option two may allow withdrawal of your Notice of Federal Tax Lien if you have entered in or converted your regular installment agreement to a direct debit installment agreement. General eligibility includes:

- You are a qualifying taxpayer (*i.e.*, individuals, businesses with income tax liability only, and out-of-business entities with any type of tax debt).

- You owe $25,000 or less (If you owe more than $25,000, you may pay down the balance to $25,000 prior to requesting withdrawal of the Notice of Federal Tax Lien).

- Your Direct Debit Installment Agreement must full pay the amount you owe within 60 months or before the Collection Statute expires, whichever is earlier.

- You are in full compliance with other filing and payment requirements.

- You must have made three consecutive direct debit payments.

- You can't have defaulted on your current, or any previous, Direct Debit Installment agreement.

How a Lien Affects You

- Assets.
  A lien attaches to all of your assets (such as property, securities, and vehicles) and to future assets acquired during the duration of the lien.

- Credit.
  Once the IRS files a Notice of Federal Tax Lien, it may limit your ability to get credit.

- Business.
  The lien attaches to all business property and to all rights to

business property, including accounts receivable.

- Bankruptcy.
  If you file for bankruptcy, your tax debt, lien, and Notice of Federal Tax Lien may continue after the bankruptcy.

Avoiding a Lien

You can avoid a federal tax lien by simply filing and paying all your taxes in full and on time. If you can't file or pay on time, don't ignore the letters or correspondence you get from the IRS.

If you can't pay the full amount you owe, payment options are available to help you settle your tax debt over time.

The Top 10 Worst Excuses for Late Tax Returns

1. *My tax return was on my yacht, which caught fire.*

2. *A wasp in my car caused me to have an accident and my tax return, which was inside, was destroyed.*

3. *My wife helps me with my tax return, but she had a headache for ten days.*

4. *My dog ate my tax return...and all the reminders.*

5. *I couldn't complete my tax return, because my husband left me and took our accountant with him.*

6. *I am currently trying to find a new accountant. My child scribbled all over the tax return, so I couldn't send it back.*

7. *I work for myself, but a colleague borrowed my tax return to photocopy it and lost it.*

8. *My husband told me the deadline was April 30th.*

9. *The postman doesn't deliver to my house.*

10. *I don't have the money.*

Chapter 8

How do I pay the IRS what don't have?

They want more than I got. Can you get blood from a stone?

If you don't pay your tax in full when you file your tax return, you'll receive a bill for the amount you owe. This bill starts the collection process, which continues until your account is satisfied or until the IRS may no longer legally collect the tax; for example, when the time or period for collection expires.

The first notice you receive will be a letter that explains the balance due and demands payment in full. It will include the amount of the tax, plus any penalties and interest accrued on your unpaid balance from the date the tax was due.

The unpaid balance is subject to daily compounding interest and a monthly late payment penalty. It's in your best interest to pay your tax liability in full as soon as you can to minimize the penalty and interest charges.

You may want to investigate and consider other methods of financing full payment of your taxes, such as obtaining a cash advance on your credit card or getting a bank loan. Often, the rate and any applicable fees your credit card company or bank charges are lower than the combination of interest and penalties imposed by the Internal Revenue Code.

If you're not able to pay your balance in full immediately, the IRS may be able to offer you a monthly installment agreement.

In some cases, you can establish an installment agreement by using the Online Payment Agreement Application (OPA), or you may complete Form 9465, *Installment Agreement Request,* and mail it in with your bill. You may also request an installment agreement over the phone by calling the phone number listed on your balance due notice. There's a user fee to set up a monthly installment agreement.

Direct debit installment agreements offer a lower user fee than other installment agreements and help you avoid defaulting on your agreement by allowing timely payments automatically. To have the payment directly debited from your bank account, complete lines 13a and 13b of Form 9465. Interest and late payment penalties will continue to accrue while you make installment payments.

If you're not able to pay the tax you owe by your original filing due date, the balance is subject to interest and a monthly late payment penalty. There's also a penalty for failure to file a tax return, so you should file timely even if you can't pay your balance in full. It's always in your best interest to pay in full as soon as you can to minimize the additional charges. If you can't pay in full, you should send in as much of the payment as you can with the notice and explore other payment arrangements. This can be done electronically or by mail.

Paying electronically is a convenient way to pay your federal taxes online, by phone, or from a mobile device. Electronic payment options are available on the IRS payments page and through the IRS2Go app. You can schedule your payment in advance, and you'll receive confirmation after it's submitted. IRS Direct Pay is a secure service that lets you pay directly from your checking or savings account at no cost to you.

You can use Direct Pay to pay your current and prior year 1040 series tax returns and more. You'll receive instant confirmation after you submit your payment. Direct Pay lets you use a "Look Up a Payment" feature to view your payment status. You can modify or cancel your payment there until two business days before your scheduled payment date.

If you decide to pay by mail, enclose a check or money order with a copy of your tax return or notice. Make it payable to the United States Treasury and provide your name, address, daytime phone number, social security number, tax year, and form number (*e.g.*, 2016 Form 1040) on the front of your payment.

Full Payment Agreements

If you can't pay in full immediately, you may qualify for additional time (up to 120 days) to pay in full. There's no fee for this full payment agreement; however, interest and any applicable penalties continue to accrue until your liability is paid in full. You may be able to set up this agreement using the Online Payment Agreement

(OPA) application or by calling the IRS at 800-829-1040 (individuals) or 800-829-4933 (businesses).

Installment Agreements

If you're not able to pay your balance in full immediately *or* within 120 days, you may still qualify for a monthly installment agreement, which allows you to make a series of monthly payments over time. To request an installment agreement, use the OPA application or complete Form 9465, *Installment Agreement Request,* and mail it to the IRS. The IRS offers the following options for making monthly payments:

- Direct debit from your bank account.

- Payroll deduction from your employer.

- Payment by Electronic Federal Tax Payment System (EFTPS).

- Payment by credit card via phone or Internet.

- Payment via check or money order.

- Payment with cash at a retail partner.

The IRS charges a user fee of $225 when you enter into a standard installment agreement or a payroll deduction agreement. If you enter a standard installment agreement and choose to pay via direct debit from your bank account, the user fee is $107. If you use the OPA application to request an installment agreement, the user fee is $149.

If you use the OPA application to request an installment agreement and choose to pay via direct debit, the user fee is $31 for all taxpayers regardless of income levels. The user fee for restructuring or reinstating an established installment agreement is $89 regardless of method of payment.

Taxpayers with income at or below 250% of the Department of Health and Human Services' poverty guidelines may apply for a reduced user fee of $43 for entering into a new installment agreement or restructuring or reinstating an established installment agreement. You can request the reduced fee by using Form 13844, *Application For Reduced User Fee For Installment Agreements.*

- If you haven't filed your return yet, you may submit Form 9465 or attach a written request for a payment plan with the monthly payment amount and due date to the front of your return.

- If you have filed your tax return and can't pay in full, you may request an installment agreement for your current tax liabilities using the OPA application. Even if the IRS hasn't yet issued you a bill, you may establish a pre-assessed agreement by entering the balance you'll owe from your tax return or notice of deficiency when prompted by OPA.

- If you can't pay in full after receiving a bill from the IRS, you may request an installment agreement using the OPA application. You also may submit Form 9465 or attach a written request for a payment plan to the front of your bill.

- You may also request an installment agreement by calling the toll-free number on your bill, or, if you don't have a bill, call the IRS at 800-829-1040 (individuals) or 800-829-4933 (businesses).

Before your installment agreement request can be considered, you must be current on all filing and payment requirements. Taxpayers in an open bankruptcy proceeding aren't eligible. You must specify the amount you can pay and the day of the month. Base your monthly installment payment amount on what you're able to pay and choose an amount you can pay each month to avoid defaulting.

Your payment date can be any day of the month from the 1st to the 28th. The IRS expects to receive your payment **on** the date you indicate, so be sure to calculate mailing time (10 days) into the date you select.

Usually, within 30 days, the IRS will respond to your request to advise you if they have approved it, denied it, or need more information.

Direct Debit and Payroll Deduction

Installment agreements via direct debit and payroll deduction enable you to make timely payments automatically and reduce the possibility of default. These convenient payment methods also allow you to avoid the time and expense of mailing monthly payments.

For a direct debit installment agreement, you must provide your checking account number, your bank routing number, and written authorization to initiate the automated withdrawal of the payment. Apply by using the OPA application, contacting IRS by phone or in person (by appointment only), or mailing Form 9465 to the IRS with your checking account number and bank routing number.

For a payroll deduction installment agreement, submit Form 2159, *Payroll Deduction Agreement.* Your employer must complete Form 2159 because a payroll deduction is an agreement between you, your employer, and the IRS. In some situations, the IRS may set up a regular installment agreement for you and convert it to a payroll deduction agreement upon receipt of the completed Form 2159 from your employer.

Offer in Compromise

If you can't fully pay under an installment agreement, you may propose an offer in compromise (OIC). An OIC is an agreement between a taxpayer and the IRS that resolves a taxpayer's tax liability through payment of an agreed upon reduced amount. Before an offer can be considered, all filing and payment requirements must be current. Taxpayers in an open bankruptcy proceeding aren't eligible. To determine OIC eligibility, you may use the Offer in Compromise Pre-Qualifier tool.

If you need more time to pay, you may ask that the Service delay collection and report your account as currently not collectible. If the IRS determines that you can't pay any of your tax debt due to a financial hardship, the IRS may temporarily delay collection by reporting your account as currently not collectible until your financial condition improves.

Being currently not collectible doesn't mean the debt goes away; it only means the IRS has determined you can't afford to pay the debt at this time.

Prior to approving your request to delay collection, the IRS may ask you to complete a Collection Information Statement (Form 433-F, Form 433-A, or Form 433-B) and provide proof of your financial status (this may include information about your assets and your monthly income and expenses). If there is a delay in collecting from you, your debt continues to accrue penalties and interest until the debt is paid in full.

The IRS may temporarily suspend certain collection actions, such as issuing a levy (explained below), until your financial condition improves. However, they may still file a Notice of Federal Tax Lien while your account is suspended. Call the phone number listed on your bill to discuss this option.

It's important to make arrangements to pay the tax due voluntarily. If you don't, as discussed, actions may be taken to collect the taxes. For example:

1) Filing a Notice of Federal Tax Lien (see chapter 7),

2) Serving a Notice of Levy (see chapter 7), or

3) Offsetting a refund to which you're entitled.

A federal tax lien is a legal claim to your property, including property that you acquire after the lien arises. The federal tax lien arises automatically when you fail to pay in full the taxes you owe within 10 days after the IRS makes an assessment of the tax and sends the first notice of taxes owed and demand for payment.

The IRS may also file a Notice of Federal Tax Lien in the public records, which publicly notifies your creditors that the IRS has a claim against all your property, including property acquired by you after the filing of the Notice of Federal Tax Lien.

The filing of a Notice of Federal Tax Lien may appear on your credit report and may harm your credit rating. Once a lien arises, the IRS generally can't release the lien until the tax, penalty, interest, and recording fees are paid in full or until the IRS may no longer legally collect the tax.

The IRS will withdraw a Notice of Federal Tax Lien if the notice was filed while a bankruptcy automatic stay was in effect. The IRS may withdraw a Notice of Federal Tax Lien if the IRS determines any of the following:

1. The Notice was filed too soon or not according to IRS procedures;

2. You enter into an installment agreement to satisfy the liability unless the installment agreement provides otherwise;

3. Withdrawal will allow you to pay your taxes more quickly; or

4. Withdrawal is in your best interest, as determined by the National Taxpayer Advocate, and in the best interest of the government.

Now What Is an Offer in Compromise?

An offer in compromise allows you to settle your tax debt for less than the full amount you owe. It may be a legitimate option if you can't pay your full tax liability or if doing so creates a financial hardship. The IRS considers ability to pay, income, expenses, and asset equity when assessing whether to approve an OIC.

The IRS generally approves an offer in compromise when the amount offered represents the most they can expect to collect within a reasonable period of time. Explore all other payment options before submitting an offer in compromise. The program is not for everyone. Finally, if you hire a tax professional to help you file an OIC, be sure to check his or her qualifications.

Making Sure You Are Eligible

Before the IRS can consider your offer, you must be current with all filing and payment requirements. You are not eligible if you are in an open bankruptcy proceeding.

Use the Offer in Compromise Pre-Qualifier tool to confirm your eligibility and prepare a preliminary proposal.

Submitting Your Offer

You'll find step-by-step instructions and all the forms for submitting an offer in the Offer in Compromise Booklet, Form 656-B. Your completed offer package will include the following:

- Form 433-A (OIC) (for individuals) or 433-B (OIC) (for businesses) and all required documentation as specified on the forms;

- Form 656(s)—Individual and business tax debt (corporation/LLC/partnership) must be submitted on separate Forms 656;

- $186 application fee (non-refundable); and

- An initial payment (non-refundable) for each Form 656.

Selecting a Payment Option

Your initial payment will vary based on your offer and the payment option you choose. You have the following two choices.

- Lump sum cash. Submit an initial payment of 20% of the total offer amount with your application. Wait for written acceptance by the IRS, then pay the remaining balance of the offer in five or fewer payments.

- Periodic payment. Submit your initial payment with your application. Continue to pay the remaining balance in monthly installments while the IRS considers your offer. If the offer is accepted, continue to pay monthly until it is paid in full.

If you meet the Low-Income Certification guidelines, located in the IRS's instructions for an offer in compromise, you do not have to send the application fee or the initial payment and you will not need to make monthly installments during the evaluation of your offer.

Understanding the Process

While your offer is being evaluated, the following things occur or may occur:

- Your non-refundable payments and fees are applied to the tax liability (you may designate payments to a specific tax year and tax debt);

- A Notice of Federal Tax Lien may be filed;

- Other collection activities are suspended;

- The legal assessment and collection period is extended;

- You make all required payments associated with your offer;

- You are not required to make payments on an existing installment agreement; and

- Your offer is automatically accepted if the IRS does not make a determination within two years of the IRS receipt date.

An IRS offer in compromise is available to virtually anyone who owes the IRS back taxes. But it is important to avoid confusing the program's widespread availability with success in getting your offer accepted.

After all, the last thing you want to do is waste time and money with the IRS on an offer that has no chance.

The offer in compromise program does work—but only in the right situation. To have success with an IRS compromise, you have to understand the IRS guidelines for analyzing your offer.

When to Avoid an Offer in Compromise

Consider: Is there a point where you could earn too much money to get a compromise accepted, and as a result have to consider other options with the IRS (installment agreements, tax bankruptcy)? There are two rules to follow when considering how your income could affect the success of your offer in compromise:

1) **The IRS has no set rules that limit an offer in compromise to certain income levels.**

There are no earnings caps to the availability of an offer in compromise. Whether you make $25,000 or $250,000, the IRS compromise guidelines will not, by themselves, make you ineligible for settlement.

2) **However, the IRS does have living expense guidelines that limit how much you can spend to get to "yes" in a compromise.**

Sure, the IRS says, go ahead and make $250,000; but if you spend it in a way that differs from what the IRS guidelines permit, your offer in compromise could run into trouble.

The IRS determines the amount of your settlement by figuring out how much they think they can collect from your cash flow over the time they have to collect your tax debt from you. The IRS defines cash flow as your earnings less your monthly living expenses (remembering that the IRS has guidelines that limit your living expenses).

The IRS has 10 years to collect a debt from you; beginning on the date you initially owed the IRS the money.

If your monthly cash flow, after being multiplied by the number of months the IRS has left to collect the debt from you, is less than what you owe, then you are in the game for an offer in compromise.

If your monthly cash flow, as defined by the IRS, can pay, in full, what you owe, then your offer will be rejected. But here is the

127

catch in getting to your monthly cash flow: The IRS will apply its living expense guidelines to your offer in compromise, and the result is often a disallowance of some of your expenses. They have limits, called IRS Collection Financial Standards that can spin your budget around and leave you with an ability to pay that is much greater than what you think it is.

In other words, the IRS cash flow analysis creates phantom cash flow—money the IRS thinks you should have to pay them, but you don't.

You don't have the money because you are spending it on living expenses. But those living expenses are slashed by the IRS in their compromise analysis, leaving you with cash flow that you don't really have, but the IRS says you should.

In an offer in compromise, it is often your world versus the IRS's world. You need to fit into the IRS's world to have success settling your tax debt with an offer in compromise.

Here is an example of some of the IRS Collection Financial Standards and how they can create phantom cash flow and increase the value of your offer in compromise,

- $1,513/month: This is what the IRS will allow a family of four for groceries, clothing, eating out, travel, entertainment, going to the movies, haircuts--in other words, monthly living expenses.

- $1,942/month: The monthly amount the IRS allows for housing and utilities (rent, mortgage payment, gas/electric, cable, internet, phone, water, trash) for a family of four living in Cincinnati, Ohio. (This amount varies based on where you live.)

- $295/month: The IRS allowance for monthly auto operating expenses (gas, maintenance, insurance) if you live in Los Angeles, California. Double it to $590/month for two cars. This amount can be higher or lower based on your locale.

- $517/month: If you spend more than $517 per month on a car payment, forget it. The IRS will only allow up to $517 per taxpayer; the excess you are paying is considered money you can pay to the IRS.

- $60/month: Medical expenses the IRS will automatically allow per member of your household—for prescriptions, doctor visits, well care, and so on. If you pay more than this, the IRS will allow it, but you will have to verify the expense.

Other expenses the IRS will allow include all of your health insurance (must be verified), a reasonable amount for life insurance (usually $200 and under), your child care/day care, a percentage of a payment plan on state or local tax back tax debts, all of your child support or alimony payments, and student loans for your education.

Expenses the IRS will not allow in an offer in compromise include any expense over the Collection Financial Standards listed above, payments on credit cards, private school tuition, college expenses for a dependent, and charitable contributions, to name a few.

Sometimes, the IRS can be persuaded to deviate from their guidelines. For example, if you drive a distance to work that requires a gas expense more than the IRS Collection Financial

Standard allows for, the IRS may be lenient in allowing it. Private education for a special needs student could likewise be permissible.

But in general, the IRS Collection Financial Standard expense limitations could create a cash flow scenario that significantly raises the value of your compromise from the phantom cash flow the IRS will attribute to you.

It's not what you make that matters in an offer in compromise as much as what you spend.

Thus, an offer can be done at higher income levels, but it becomes more dependent on items like child support (which is allowed in full) eating up your cash flow rather than your other living expenses (which will be limited and create phantom cash flow). For these reasons, at higher income levels, the IRS analysis is geared to make compromising more difficult.

If your cash flow, whether real or phantom, results in the IRS determining that they can get paid in full over the remaining time left to collect from you, your compromise will be rejected. There would be no need to waste time with an offer in compromise; a better plan would be alternative remedies like a payment plan over the remaining collection time period, or possibly even filing for bankruptcy.

Other Options

There are times where you agree with the IRS that you owe taxes, but you can't pay due to your current financial situation. If the IRS agrees that you can't both pay your taxes and your reasonable living expenses, it may place your account in Currently Not Collectible (CNC) (hardship) status.

While your account is in CNC status, the IRS will not generally engage in collection activity (for example, it won't levy on your assets and income). However, the IRS will still charge interest and penalties to your account, and may keep your refunds and apply them to your debt.

Before the IRS will place your account in CNC status, it may ask you to file any delinquent tax returns. If you request CNC status, the IRS may ask you to provide financial information, including your income and expenses, and whether you can sell any assets or get a loan.

If your account is placed in CNC status, during the time it can collect the debt, the IRS may review your income annually to see if your situation has improved. Generally, the IRS can attempt to collect your taxes up to 10 years from the date they were assessed, though the 10-year period is suspended in certain cases. The time the suspension is in effect will extend the time the IRS has to collect the tax.

Because the IRS won't suspend interest and penalty charges, even if it stops trying to collect the balance due, you may want to consider other possible payment options within your means before asking the IRS to place your account in CNC status.

Actions to Take

Don't ignore notices you get from the IRS about balances due.

If you decide to request currently not collectible (CNC) status, you should take the following actions:

- File tax returns for prior years (if you were required to file a return).

- Continue to file your returns on time even if you can't pay. This will prevent late filing penalties.

- Gather your information to verify your income, expenses, and any debts you owe on your assets (loans). You may need to provide the IRS this financial information so it can decide whether to grant your request.

To see if you qualify for CNC status, you'll need to contact the IRS. If you got a notice, use the information included there. If you don't have or have lost your notice, call the following toll free numbers for assistance:

- Individual taxpayers: 800-829-1040 (or TTY/TDD 800-829-4059)

- Business taxpayers: 800-829-4933

If the IRS decides you can make some type of payment and you still disagree, you may take the following actions:

- Request a conference with the IRS Collection Manager. IRS employees are required to give you the name and phone number of their supervisor.

- Hire an attorney, CPA, or EA to represent you. If your income is below a certain level, you may qualify for assistance from a Low Income Taxpayer Clinic.

- Appeal certain collection actions the IRS is taking or proposing. See IRS Publication 1660, *Collection Appeal Rights*.

While applying for CNC status, the following things may happen:

- The IRS may ask you to file any delinquent returns.

- The IRS may ask you to complete IRS Form 433-A, *Collection Information Statement for Wage Earners and Self-Employed Individuals*, or IRS Form 433-F, *Collection Information Statement, and/or IRS Form 433B, Collection Information Statement for Businesses*, before making any collection decision.

- The IRS may require documentation to support items listed on your Collection Information Statement.

- The IRS will continue to charge monthly late payment penalties and interest on your account.

If the IRS places your account in currently not collectable status, the following conditions apply:

- The IRS may keep your tax refunds and apply them to your debt.

- You can still make voluntary payments.

- The IRS should not levy your assets or income.

- The IRS may file a Notice of Federal Tax Lien even if your account is placed in CNC status.

- The IRS may contact you to update your financial information to be sure your ability to pay hasn't changed.

What If I Still Can't Pay in the Future?

If your account is placed in CNC status and the IRS sends you a notice about your tax bill, call the number on the notice to discuss your financial situation.

The IRS will take your updated information and decide if you can pay. Make sure you collect all the information about your income and expenses before you call.

Prevent future tax liabilities by adjusting your withholding or making estimated tax payments.

Top 10 Mistakes on Tax Returns

1. They do not sign the return

2. The basic information is incorrect

3. They don't enter income as it's been reported to them (and the IRS)

4. They enter items on the wrong line

5. They automatically claim the standard deduction

6. They don't take write-offs they are entitled to

7. They don't check for typos

8. They report negative numbers incorrectly

9. They don't pay their taxes properly

10. They don't bother telling the IRS how to handle their refund

Chapter 9

How do you get the IRS off your back, temporarily?

What Stops the Internal Revenue Service from Collecting?

The IRS cannot collect from you, attempt to collect from you, or attempt to audit you forever. Conversely, you cannot get refunds forever, either. These time limits are called statutes of limitations (SOLs). An SOL is, in this situation, a time period established by law in which the IRS must review, analyze, and resolve tax issues.

The Internal Revenue Code requires that the Service assess, refund, credit, or collect taxes within a specified period of time; otherwise, these actions are prohibited. Several of the specific statutes are discussed in this chapter.

Assessment Statute Expiration Date

The Assessment Statute Expiration Date (ASED) is the time frame that the IRS can assess a tax, penalties, or interest on a filed return.

The ASED is generally three years from the date the return was filed. For example: You file your personal return (form 1040, 1040A, or 1040EZ) on or before April 15th (or that year's tax return due date).

Therefore, the ASED expires on the April 15th (or that year's tax return due date) three years into the future, even if you file the return earlier. If you file it later and you filed an extension, your ASED expires three years from that date. If filed later, an extension is mandatory. Returns are not automatically extended unless the extension form is **timely** filed by the **original** due date.

Refund Statute Expiration Date

The Refund Statute Expiration date (RSED) is the time frame that the taxpayer can request a refund by filing an original return, an amended return, or another "claim for refund". The RSED is split into two timeframes. Like an ASED, it is also generally three years from the date the return was filed, or two years from the date the tax was paid.

If the claim for a credit or refund is not filed within the three-year period required for filing for a refund, the amount is limited to the portion of tax paid (the payment of tax could be for tax, penalty, or interest) within the two-year period immediately preceding the filing of the claim. Following is an example of the two-year-rule regarding claims for credit or refund.

For tax year 2012, Taxpayer files a tax return and pays $5,500 of individual income tax on April 15, 2013. On March 1, 2016, Taxpayer pays $1,500 as a result of an examination that increased their rental income. The ASED was not extended (which is an option when dealing with an audit), and expires on April 15, 2016. On May 1, 2016, the taxpayer files a refund claim for $2,000 to dispute the audit adjustment. The taxpayer may receive only a $1,500 refund (which is the amount of the audit tax adjustment, as indicated above) under the two-year rule.

Collection Statute Expiration Date

The Collection Statute Expiration Date (CSED) is a 10-year period during which the IRS can try to collect on a tax debt.

Though this book deals only with IRS rules, I would be remiss not to mention that your state or local government will have their own SOLs. They may mirror the Internal Revenue Code, but then again, they may not.

Extending a Statute

Can anything extend these statutes? The short answer is yes. If the filed return is determined to have understated more than 25% of the actual income received (and it was not because of fraud), the ASED is extended to six years.

If the taxpayer files a false or fraudulent return with the intent to evade paying the appropriate amount of tax or if there is a willful attempt to evade taxes, the statute is indefinite.

The statute also does not start until a return is actually filed.

There are other ways to extend the time period in which the IRS can collect beyond the 10-year CSED. These are referred to as "tolling of the statutes." According to Wikipedia, "Tolling is a legal doctrine which allows for the pausing or delaying of the running of the period of time set forth by a statute of limitations."

The following actions toll the statutes.

1. **Offer in compromise.**

   Filing an offer in compromise will extend the statute of limitations on collection by the time it is pending plus 30 days. The IRS can take six to twelve months to investigate an offer in compromise, and if it is accepted, the IRS will allow you up to two years to pay the settlement amount. Submitting an offer is not always in your best interest. See the section on Offers in Compromise in chapter 8 for more information.

2. **A Collection Due Process appeal.**

   Timely responding to an IRS Final Notice of Intent to Levy, known as a Collection Due Process hearing, will extend the time the IRS has to collect while your hearing is pending.

3. **Bankruptcy.**

   Bankruptcy extends the statute of limitations on collection by the time you were in bankruptcy plus six months. If you filed bankruptcy but did not eliminate all of your tax liabilities, the IRS will have more time to collect the non-discharged taxes from you.

4. **Innocent spouse relief.**

The collection period is suspended from the filing of the request for innocent spouse relief until the 90-day period for petitioning the Tax Court expires. If a Tax Court petition is filed on an IRS denial, time is tolled until the Tax Court decision becomes final plus 60 days.

5. **Taxpayer Assistance Order (Form 911).**

If communications break down to the point of you needing a Taxpayer Assistance Order to stop the IRS, filing Form 911 will suspend the statute of limitations on collection while your case is pending review.

6. **Installment agreements.**

If the IRS refuses or defaults on an installment agreement, you have the right to appeal that decision. If you do, the collection timeframe is extended during the appeal.

The IRS gets more time because these actions prevent them from collecting from you.

What the IRS gives you—no enforced collection activity (*i.e.*, no notices or levies)—they get back. You may ask why someone would want to extend the statute. That is where a professional experienced in IRS collection issues will guide you.

Divorcing your spouse does not mean you are divorcing their tax problems.

Chapter 10

I'm Innocent, I Tell You. I Didn't Do It.
Having a Tax Debt That Isn't Yours

Getting in trouble for other peoples' money

Let's say you are getting married and you marry into a tax disaster. If you file a joint return, you are individually and severally liable. That means that no matter whose income is reported, you both are responsible for the debt. There are a couple options to avoid this.

One is filing as married filing separately (different from filing as single) instead of married filing jointly. Another option is to file as head of household. This option applies if you live apart from your spouse for the last six months of the tax year, are still married, but have a *minor* dependent child living with you.

Otherwise, if you file jointly and are expecting a refund, but your spouse has a prior tax debt, the IRS will hold the current refund and apply it against the tax debt, even your part. An option for avoiding this is called filing an <u>injured spouse claim</u>. You will claim that part of the refund in the current year should be applied against a debt that has nothing to do with you. An injured spouse claim can cover other non-tax debts as well (such as student loans).

Now, what if you were audited related to a jointly filed return, and the Revenue Agent or Revenue Officer finds that the return did not include a significant amount of income that your spouse failed to report? You are responsible because you filed jointly with your spouse. If you find yourself in this situation, there is a three-part Internal Revenue Code section (§6015) called Innocent Spouse that deals with this situation. Making this claim is not as easy as it sounds.

> 1st, the claim has to be made within two years of the filing of the return.

> 2nd, you had to have no reason to know of or benefit from not paying the tax. It is a lot more complicated that, but that is where an experienced EA or CPA can assist you.

Substitutes for Return

There are times when you may get a notice that says that you owe taxes, penalties, and interest or a return that is (for example) 15 years old. You are shocked, as you do not remember filing a return way back then.

Other than the possibility of identity theft, a return may also have been prepared for you.

Who would do that? The IRS, that's who.

The Code allows for the IRS to file a return on behalf of a delinquent taxpayer. These are called substitutes for return (SFRs). SFRs are generally filed two to six years after the due date of the return.

These returns are returns for the express purpose of collecting a tax debt. Therefore, the 10-year collection statute clock starts to tick. However, it starts with the date the tax was posted (or assessed) to your tax account, not the due date for the year in question. Remember, these returns can be filed several years after the "normal" due date.

The returns are prepared in the worst possible light. If the last return filed has you listed as married and the IRS has no reason to believe that you are not, they will use the "married filing separate" status. They will not allow for any dependents, will not compute any credits, and do not allow for any deductions like mortgage interest, real estate taxes, or stock basis on investment sales.

So what happens when the IRS "prepares" an SFR? You will not be notified when this happens. You only find out when you get a tax bill for a return that you know you did not file. Many times, when I am dealing with one issue for a client, I notice that an SFR was prepared when I request a client's account transcript.

Scuttling the ship
When all else fails, you may be able to bankrupt it
out.

Chapter 11

Can you really start over and get a second chance?

Bankruptcy. The final frontier to get clear.

It is possible to file bankruptcy and have your past due taxes eliminated. If your credit is bad and you have other non-tax debts, you need to consult with an attorney before taking this step.

Like everything else when it comes to taxes, things are not that simple. In many cases, including in family law and bankruptcy law, the Internal Revenue Code trumps bankruptcy law. That means that even if a court discharges the tax debt, the IRS does not have to agree to it. They can continue to seek payment.

If you have filed a return late or if an SFR has been filed on your behalf, many district courts have ruled that the taxes associated with these returns are not dischargeable.

If you think bankruptcy is a serious option for you, then you need to see a lawyer who specializes in this field.

I discuss the different types of bankruptcy filings below. I am not an attorney. This part of the book is general knowledge, available anywhere for the public to read. I am just trying to make it easier to understand.

In a Chapter 7 bankruptcy…

> all of your property that is non-exempt (*i.e.*, generally anything in your primary residence) is liquidated to pay the debt(s).

In a Chapter 13 bankruptcy…

> eligible individuals pay part or all of their debts over a period of time, usually three to five years.

In a Chapter 11 bankruptcy…

> the debtor proposes a plan (called a "reorganization plan"), and must get approval from their creditors. If the debt is related to taxes owed, the debt must be paid within five years. This option is usually used by individuals with big debts and by companies. It is a very costly option due to large legal fees and other costs.

In a Chapter 12 bankruptcy...

> eligible farmers pay part or all of their debts over a
> period of time, usually three to five years.

In layman's terms, the types of bankruptcy can be described as
follows:

- Chapter 7
  They discharge your debt, but they take your stuff.

- Chapter 13
  You keep your stuff, but must make payments of part of
  your debt over three to five years, after which you get a
  discharge of the balance due.

- Chapter 11
  You keep your stuff, make payments. Usually used for
  large debts and is costly.

- Chapter 12
  Farmers. Enough said.

All federal, state, and local tax returns must be filed after your case
starts. Failure to timely or, at the very least, file a current extension
may cause you to place in a less favorable chapter or have the case
dismissed in its entirety.

Chapter 13 filers must file all required returns for tax years within
four years of filing the bankruptcy petition. The filing of the
returns is a bankruptcy court requirement. It has nothing to do with
having the tax debt, if there is any, to be discharged. It is to
discharge everything else.

What happens if you owe individual income taxes?
Can all these taxes be discharged?

Well, the bankruptcy courts may say yes, but the IRS may say no. In my years of experience, most bankruptcy attorneys do not understand the nuances of when taxes can be or cannot be discharged. I have more clients come to me that I would like saying that they filed bankruptcy and all their taxes should be discharged—so why are they receiving a notice of taxes due, plus penalties and interest?

When can you discharge (wipe out) your individual income tax debt?

You can discharge debt for federal income taxes in Chapter 7 bankruptcy only if *all* of the following conditions are true:

- **You filed a tax return.**

  You must have filed a tax return for the debt you wish to discharge at least two years before filing for bankruptcy. (In most courts, if you file a late return, meaning your extensions have expired and the IRS filed a substitute return on your behalf, you have not filed a "return" and cannot discharge the tax. In some courts, you can discharge tax debt that is the subject of a late return as long as you meet the other criteria.)

- **The return was due at least three years ago.**

  The tax debt must be disclosed on a tax return that was due (including all valid extensions) at least three years before you filed for bankruptcy. For example, if you disclosed the taxes in a 2005 income tax return for which extensions to file the return expired on October 15, 2006, you will satisfy the tax return due date test if you file the bankruptcy petition after October 15, 2009.

- **You filed the return at least two years ago.**

You must have filed the tax return at least two years before filing for bankruptcy. In most courts, a late return does not count as a "return," and you won't be able to discharge the taxes (late means your extensions have expired and the IRS filed a substitute return on your behalf). In other courts, you can discharge tax debt even if you file a late return, assuming you meet the other criteria.

- **The taxes were assessed at least 240 days ago.**

The taxing authority must have assessed (entered the liability on the taxing authority's records) the tax against you at least 240 days before you filed for bankruptcy. This time limit may be extended if you have an offer in compromise with the taxing authority or you had previously filed for bankruptcy.

- **You did not commit fraud or willful evasion of taxes.**

The tax return must not be fraudulent or frivolous and you cannot be guilty of any intentional act of evading the tax laws. If you file a joint petition, the taxing authority must prove that both you and your spouse committed an act of fraud related to the applicable return or willfully attempted to evade the tax.

For the most part, income taxes are the only type of tax debt that is non-priority debt in Chapter 13 bankruptcy. This means your tax debt must be for federal or state income taxes or taxes on gross receipts and meet the following conditions.

There are other alternatives before you file bankruptcy and the IRS does not always accept the bankruptcy courts' decision.

This is not a time or place to shortcut or attempt to fast track a quick fix.

The Dirty Dozen Worst of the Worst Tax Scams

1. *Phishing:*
Taxpayers need to be on guard against fake emails or websites looking to steal personal information.

2. *Phone Scams:*
Phone calls from criminals impersonating IRS agents remain an ongoing threat to taxpayers.

3. *Identity Theft:*
Taxpayers need to watch out for identity theft especially around tax time.

4. *Return Preparer Fraud:*
Be on the lookout for unscrupulous return preparers.

5. *Fake Charities:*
Be on guard against groups masquerading as charitable organizations to attract donations from unsuspecting contributors.

6. *Inflated Refund Claims:*
   Taxpayers should be on the lookout for anyone promising inflated refunds

7. *Excessive Claims for Business Credits:*
   Avoid improperly claiming the fuel tax credit, a tax benefit generally not available to most taxpayers

8. *Falsely Padding Deductions on Returns:*
   Taxpayers should avoid the temptation to falsely inflate deductions or expenses on their returns to pay less than what they owe or potentially receive larger refunds.

9. *Falsifying Income to Claim Credits:*
   Don't invent income to erroneously qualify for tax credits, such as the Earned Income Tax Credit.

10. *Abusive Tax Shelters:*
    Don't use abusive tax structures to avoid paying taxes.

11. *Frivolous Tax Arguments:*
    Don't use frivolous tax arguments to avoid paying tax.

12. *Offshore Tax Avoidance:*

The recent string of successful enforcement actions against offshore tax cheats and the financial organizations that help them shows that it's a bad bet to hide money and income offshore.

Chapter 12

Private collectors and other problems outside of the IRS

Scary and confusing letters still coming? If not the IRS than who?

Private Debt Collectors

You may have heard that the IRS has decided to bring back an unsuccessful former program where by private debt collectors will attempt to collect on certain tax debts from certain taxpayers. Usually, the tax professional community will tell clients that the IRS will not call taxpayers and ask them to pay their debt, in full. However, the Service has contracted with four independent companies (see the Agencies Selected section) that will call taxpayers and ask them, usually directly over the phone, to pay their debt.

This can be fraught with problems, including the possibility of identity theft, which is discussed in the Identity Theft section. The

Service says that these companies will identify themselves with specific identification numbers. However, many scams are being put forth doing this exact same thing.

In any case, you need to be aware of this private debt collection program. As stated on the IRS website, the program, authorized under a federal law enacted by Congress, enables these designated contractors to collect, on the government's behalf, outstanding tax debt. A federal law, Fixing America's Surface Transportation Act (FAST Act), requires the IRS to use these agencies.

As a condition of receiving a contract, these agencies must respect taxpayer rights including, among other things, abiding by the consumer protection provisions of the Fair Debt Collection Practices Act.

These private collection agencies will work on cold cases accounts where the IRS is no longer actively working them. Several factors contribute to the IRS assigning these accounts to private collection agencies, including older, overdue tax accounts or lack of resources preventing the IRS from working the cases.

The IRS will give taxpayers and their representative (enrolled agent, CPA, or attorney) written notice that the accounts are being transferred to the private collection agencies. The agencies will send a second, separate letter to the taxpayer and their representative confirming this transfer.

Private collection agencies will be allowed to identify themselves as contractors of the IRS collecting taxes. Private collection agencies will not ask for payment on a prepaid debit, iTunes, or gift card. Taxpayers will be informed about allowable electronic payment options on IRS.gov/Pay Your Tax Bill. Payment by check should be payable to the U.S. Treasury and sent directly to IRS, not the private collection agency.

Agencies Selected

The IRS will assign cases to the following private collection agencies (current as of August 2017):

- CBE
  P.O. Box 2217
  Waterloo, IA 50704
  1-800-910-5837

- ConServe
  P.O. Box 307
  Fairport, NY 14450-0307
  1-844-853-4875

- Performant
  P.O. Box 9045
  Pleasanton, CA 94566-9045
  1-844-807-9367

- Pioneer
  P.O. Box 500
  Horseheads, NY 14845
  1-800-448-3531

If you do not wish to work with the assigned private collection agency to settle your overdue tax account, you must submit a request in writing to the private collection agency. We suggest getting competent representation if you need to submit a request.

Accounts Not Assigned to Private Collection Agencies

IRS will not assign accounts to private collection agencies involving taxpayers who meet one or more of the following criteria:

- Deceased

- Under the age of 18

- In designated combat zones

- Victims of tax-related identity theft

- Currently under examination, litigation, criminal investigation, or levy

- Subject to pending or active offers in compromise

- Subject to an installment agreement

- Subject to a right of appeal

- Classified as innocent spouse cases

- In presidentially declared disaster areas and requesting relief from collection

Private collection agencies will return accounts to the IRS if taxpayers and their accounts fall into any of these 10 categories.

Even when dealing with private debt collection, you shouldn't receive unexpected phone calls from the IRS demanding payment.

When people owe tax, the IRS always sends several collection notices through the mail before making phone calls. However, a situation can arise where a phone call is unexpected if a tax debtor (that is, a taxpayer who is not paying their taxes) owes more than $10,000, a lien is filed, unbeknownst to the debtor.

If they accrue more tax debt, meaning over $50,000 or ignore the various notices sent, the debtor is notified that a "notice of federal tax lien" was issued. If a lien is recorded with the county, it is public information. In this way, anyone can get a lien list and start making calls demanding money. Taxpayers need to be aware as to who is calling and seek assistance from a professional tax advisor experienced in tax controversy.

Identity Theft

We all know the term. Identity theft is where someone finds our social security number, takes out credit cards, and buys to their heart's content. What many people do not realize is that an even bigger potential identity theft problem exists where taxes and tax returns are concerned. In this situation, the unscrupulous person finds your social security number, and instead of opening up credit card accounts, they file tax returns with false information and unknown dependents and get a nice refund. Most of these fraudulent tax returns deal with the Earned Income, Additional Child, and American Opportunity Tax Credits (called "refundable credits").

How widespread is this problem? As of December 31, 2015, the IRS reported that it had identified and confirmed more than one million fraudulent tax returns and prevented the issuance of nearly $6.8 billion in fraudulent tax refunds as a result of the identity theft filters. They know how many fraudulent returns they stopped, but not how many returns they did not—it's probably more than $6.8 billion worth.

You generally find out you are the victim of tax return fraud after attempting to file your return electronically and having it rejected upon submission to the IRS. The rejection code will say that a return that contains the primary, secondary, or any of the dependents were used on another return already filed. Because you are not the victim (the law says that the IRS is), you will never know who did this terrible deed. There has been talk of allowing the true taxpayer to see the return that was filed.

Does this mean you will not get your rightful refund or have your tax account credited correctly? Of course not. There are procedures in place, forms to file, and then it becomes a waiting game before you are refunded your tax money or allowed a credit to be carried over to the next year, depending on what you chose on the return.

The IRS delays the start of tax season each year because of the rash of these returns.

The IRS waits so that more information returns (W-2s, and 1099s, to name a couple) are filed with the IRS. Returns with the credits mentioned above can be filed, but the refund will be delayed by weeks, not days, in the name of protecting the public as the IRS waits for the filing of these information returns. If your tax return is severely delayed, you may wish to call your local congressional leader for help.

Being Denied a Passport

As mentioned in the Private Debt Collectors section, in late 2015, Congress passed the   FAST Act, designed to help with the collection of past-due tax debts owed to the national treasury.

Private collection agencies is just one part of this act and we covered earlier. A second component of the FAST Act is that the law now requires Departments of State to deny a passport application and allowing for it to revoke already issued passports under certain conditions.

These are:

- Your liability has been assessed. This means you filed a return that shows tax due, the IRS filed a return for you (this is called a Substitute for Return, or SFR), or the IRS conducted an audit and assessed a tax.

- The tax assessed is greater than $50,000.

- You fall under either of the following:

   o A notice of lien was filed and the right to a Collection Due Process hearing has expired;

   o A levy notice has been issued.

You must also be aware of the exceptions to the rule:

- You are currently paying your tax debt via an installment arrangement or one is pending.

- You have an offer in compromise pending.

- You are considered currently not collectible.

- You requested and were granted a Collection Due Process Hearing, but it has not happened yet. This is, as discussed in chapter 9, a tolling of the statutes. Therefore, the same guidelines apply here.

- You requested a hearing relating to being an innocent spouse.

Will the state automatically deny your application or revoke your passport in these situations? No, not exactly.

The law requires that a notice called a "contemporaneous notice" be sent to the taxpayer at or near the time the IRS declares that the debt is "seriously delinquent." In addition to this notice, notification must be included in all Collection Due Process hearing notices.

Top Ten Reasons to Hire an Enrolled Agent (EA)

1. *It gives you peace of mind knowing that an EA is taking care of it*

2. *An EA can recommend ways to save on taxes*

3. *An EA can help you plan all year and for future years*

4. *An EA can answer your questions to help you make smarter tax-saving decisions*

5. *A tax program in a box cannot represent you in an audit*

6. *Your time is worth money – add up the hours you would spend doing it yourself and calculate what that's worth*

7. *Making mistakes can be very costly*

8. *You don't have to keep up with the many tax law changes or understand complicated tax*

law

9. It takes the hassle out of doing it yourself.

10. This is what an EA does, it is not what you do.

Conclusion

Your issues might take a while.
Some assembly and patience required.

I have read the book, Now what and what comes next?

What does a person do when they owe money to the IRS and they cannot pay it? Taxpayers should retain a competent enrolled agent, certified public accountant, or attorney to act on their behalf and explain the options and alternatives. As discussed in this book, you have several options to pay the taxes you owe, whether via your own filing, the IRS filing the Substitute of Return, or an adverse audit result.

When all else fails, you can always go to court.

There is a specialty court called the United States Tax Court, composed of 19 presidentially appointed members. Those judges, senior judges serving on recall, and special trial judges conduct trial sessions and perform other work of the Court. All of the judges have expertise in tax law and apply that expertise to ensure that taxpayers are assessed only what they owe, and no more. Although the Court is physically located in Washington, D.C., the judges travel nationwide to conduct trials in various designated cities.

If you choose to go to tax court, you can go before the court yourself, which is called pro se representation; hire an attorney; or hire a a United States Tax Court Practitioner (USTCP), an individual who has passed the Tax Court Exam for Non-Attorneys, to represent you.

One of the notices previously discussed gives you 90 days to petition the court. If you miss this deadline you miss a great benefit. You, usually, do not have to pay the tax first for small cases (owes less than $50,000 for any one year.

For example, if you owe $50,000 for each of three years or $150,000, you qualify as a small case. It is a less formal procedure as there is no jury.

You or your representative (it is advisable not to do this alone) present your case, as does the IRS, through their lawyer. The downside? The losing side cannot appeal the decision.

This book's purpose has been to give you the tools you need to understand what having a tax debt can mean.

The all-encompassing advice:

Tax debt is not something to ignore.

The IRS has a long memory.

They will not forget.

And the longer you wait to take care of the problem, the harder and more costly it will be.

Appendix

Now what about some examples?

IRS List of Notices.

Notice Number	Description	Topic
CP01	We received the information that you provided and have verified your claim of identity theft. We have placed an identity theft indicator on your account.	Identity Theft
CP01A	This notice tells you about the Identity Protection Personal Identification Number (IP PIN) we sent you.	Identity Theft

CP01B	This notice tells you the IRS needs more information from you to process your tax return accurately.	Identity Theft
CP01C	This CP01C notice is issued to taxpayers who are not currently impacted by tax-related identity theft to acknowledge receipt of standard identity theft documentation and to inform them their account has been marked with an identity theft indicator.	Identity Theft
CP01E	This CP01E notice is issued to taxpayers who may be victims of identity theft because their social security number (SSN) and possibly their personal information were used for employment by someone other than the valid SSN owner.	Identity Theft
CP01H	You received a CP 01H notice because we were unable to process your tax return. The IRS has locked your account because the Social Security Administration informed us that the Social Security number (SSN) of the primary or secondary taxpayer on the return belongs to someone who was deceased prior to the tax year shown on the tax form.	SSN
CP01S	We received your Form 14039 or similar statement for your identity	Identity Theft

	theft claim. If you are due a refund, we'll issue it or contact you when we finish processing your case or if we need additional information.	
CP02H	You owe a balance due as a result of amending your tax return to show receipt of a grant received as a result of Hurricane Katrina, Rita or Wilma.	Balance Due
CP03C	You received a tax credit (called the First-Time Homebuyer Credit) for a house you purchased. You may need to file a form to report a change in ownership to the house you purchased.	Credit
CP04	Our records show that you or your spouse served in a combat zone, a qualified contingency operation, or a hazardous duty station during the tax year specified on your notice. As a result, you may be eligible for tax deferment.	Combat Zone
CP05	We sent you this notice because we're reviewing your tax return to verify income, deductions, credits, etc. We're holding your refund until we finish our review.	Verification
CP05A	We are examining your return and we need documentation.	Verification

CP05B	We issue a CP05B notice when the IRS receives a tax return that shows a refund amount and we can't determine if the income reported on the tax return matches the income reported to us by payers. The IRS is holding your refund until we receive the additional information we requested from you to determine if the income is correct before we can release your refund.	Refund
CP06	We're auditing your tax return and need documentation from you to verify the Premium Tax Credit (PTC) that you claimed. We are holding all or part of your refund, pending the result of this audit, because of this discrepancy with your PTC.	ACA
CP06A	We're auditing your tax return and need documentation from you to verify the Premium Tax Credit (PTC) that you claimed.	ACA
CP07	We received your tax return and are holding your refund until we complete a more thorough review of the benefits you claimed under a treaty and/or the deductions claimed on Schedule A.	Deductions
CP08	You may qualify for the Additional Child Tax Credit and be entitled to	Additional Child Tax

	some additional money.	Credit
CP09	We've sent you this notice because our records indicate you may be eligible for the Earned Income Tax Credit (EITC), but didn't claim it on your tax return.	EITC
CP10	We made a change(s) to your return because we believe there's a miscalculation. This change(s) affected the estimated tax payment you wanted applied to your taxes for next year.	Change To Your Estimated Tax Credit Amount
CP10A	We made a change(s) to your return because we believe there's a miscalculation involving your Earned Income Tax Credit. This change(s) affected the estimated tax payment you wanted applied to your taxes for next year.	Change To Your Estimated Tax Credit Amount
CP11	We made changes to your return because we believe there's a miscalculation. You owe money on your taxes as a result of these changes.	Balance Due
LT11	We haven't received any payment from you for your overdue taxes. This letter is to advise you of our intent to seize your property or rights to	Levy

	property. You must contact us immediately.	
ST11	No hemos recibido ningún pago de usted para sus impuestos atrasados. Esta carta es para informarle de nuestra intención de embargar sus propiedades o derechos a la propiedad. Usted debe comunicarse con nosotros inmediatamente.	Embargo
CP11A	We made changes to your return because we believe there's a miscalculation involving your Earned Income Tax Credit. You owe money on your taxes as a result of these changes.	Balance Due
CP11M	We made changes to your return involving the Making Work Pay and Government Retiree Credit. You owe money on your taxes as a result of these changes.	Balance Due
CP11R	We made changes to your return involving the Recovery Rebate Credit. You owe money on your taxes as a result of these changes.	Balance Due
CP12	We made changes to correct a miscalculation on your return.	Return Error

CP12A	We made changes to correct the Earned Income Tax Credit (EITC) claimed on your tax return.	EITC
CP12E or CP12F	We made changes to correct a miscalculation on your return.	Return Error
CP12M	We made changes to the computation of the Making Work Pay and/or Government Retiree Credits on your return.	Return Error
CP12R	We made changes to the computation of the Rebate Recovery Credit on your return.	Return Error
CP13	We made changes to your return because we believe there's a miscalculation. You're not due a refund nor do you owe an additional amount because of our changes. Your account balance is zero.	Zero Balance
CP13A	We made changes to your return because we found an error involving your Earned Income Tax Credit. You're not due a refund nor do you owe an additional amount because of our changes. Your account balance is zero.	Zero Balance
CP13M	We made changes to your return involving the Making Work Pay	Zero Balance

	credit or the Government Retiree Credit. You're not due a refund nor do you owe an additional amount because of our changes. Your account balance is zero.	
CP13R	We made changes to your return involving the Recovery Rebate Credit. You're not due a refund nor do you owe an additional amount because of our changes. Your account balance is zero.	Zero Balance
CP14	We sent you this notice because you owe money on unpaid taxes.	Balance Due
CP14 A/B/C/D/ E Notice	We sent you this notice because you owe money on unpaid taxes.	Balance Due
LT14	We show you have past due taxes and we've been unable to reach you. Call us immediately.	Balance Due
ST14	Nuestros registros indican que usted todavía adeuda impuestos morosos, y no hemos podido comunicarnos con usted. Llámenos inmediatamente.	Saldo pendiente
CP14H	We sent you this notice because you owe money on an unpaid shared responsibility payment.	ACA

CP14I	You owe taxes and penalties because you didn't take out the minimum amount you had to from your traditional individual retirement arrangement (IRA). Or, you put into a tax-sheltered account more than you can legally.	IRA
CP15B	We charged you a Trust Fund Recovery Penalty (TFRP) for not paying employment or excise taxes.	Penalty
CP15H	Your shared responsibility payment (SRP) assessment is due to a recalculation based on changes to your income tax liability. Your examination results are addressed in a separate correspondence.	ACA
CP16	We sent you this notice to tell you about changes we made to your return that affect your refund. We made these changes because we believe there was a miscalculation. Our records show you owe other tax debts and we applied all or part of your refund to them.	Refund
LT16 A/B/C/D/ E/F/G	We may take enforcement action to collect taxes you owe because you have not responded to previous notices we sent you on this matter. We need to hear from you about your	Balance Due

	overdue taxes or tax returns.	
ST16 A/B/C/D/ E/F/G	Podemos empezar acciones de cobro para cobrarle el impuesto que adeuda, ya que usted no ha respondido a los avisos anteriores que le enviamos referentes a este asunto. Tenemos que saber de usted en cuanto a sus impuestos o declaraciones morosas.	Saldo pendiente
CP18	We believe you incorrectly claimed one or more deductions or credits. As a result, your refund is less than you expected.	Refund
LT18	We have not received a response from you to our previous requests for overdue tax returns.	Balance Due
ST18	Podemos empezar acciones de cobro para cobrarle el impuesto que adeuda, ya que usted no ha respondido a los avisos anteriores que le enviamos referentes a este asunto. Tenemos que saber de usted en cuanto a sus impuestos o declaraciones morosas.	Saldo pendiente
CP19	We have increased the amount of tax you owe because we believe you incorrectly claimed one or more deductions or credits.	Deductions

CP20	We believe you incorrectly claimed one or more deductions or credits. As a result, your refund is less than you expected.	Deductions
CP21A	We made the change(s) you requested to your tax return for the tax year specified on the notice. You owe money on your taxes as a result of the change(s).	Balance Due
CP21B	We made the change(s) you requested to your tax return for the tax year specified on the notice. You should receive your refund within 2-3 weeks of your notice.	Refund
CP21C	We made the change(s) you requested to your tax return for the tax year specified on the notice. You're not due a refund nor do you owe any additional amount. Your account balance for this tax form and tax year is zero.	Even Balance
CP21E	As a result of your recent audit, we made changes to your tax return for the tax year specified on the notice. You owe money on your taxes as a result of these changes.	Balance Due
CP21H	We made the changes you requested to your tax return for the tax year on	Balance Due

	the notice, which also changed your shared responsibility payment.	
CP21I	We made changes to your tax return for the tax year specified on the notice for Individual Retirement Arrangement (IRA) taxes. You owe money on your taxes as a result of these changes.	Balance Due
CP22A	We made the change(s) you requested to your tax return for the tax year specified on the notice. You owe money on your taxes as a result of the change(s).	Balance Due
CP22E	As a result of your recent audit, we made changes to your tax return for the tax year specified on the notice. You owe money on your taxes as a result of these changes.	Balance Due
CP22H	We made the changes you requested to your tax return for the tax year on the notice, which also changed your shared responsibility payment.	Balance Due
CP22I	We made changes to your tax return for the tax year specified on the notice for Individual Retirement Arrangement (IRA) taxes. You owe money on your taxes as a result of these changes.	Balance Due

CP23	We made changes to your return because we found a difference between the amount of estimated tax payments on your tax return and the amount we posted to your account. You have a balance due because of these changes.	Balance Due
CP24	We made changes to your return because we found a difference between the amount of estimated tax payments on your tax return and the amount we posted to your account. You have a potential overpayment credit because of these changes.	Refund
LT24	We received your payment proposal to pay the tax you owe; however, we need more information about your financial situation.	Balance Due
ST24	Recibimos su propuesta de pago para pagar los impuestos que adeuda. Sin embargo, necesitamos más información acerca de su situación financiera.	Saldo pendiente
CP24E	We made changes to your return because we found a difference between the amount of estimated tax payments on your tax return and the amount we posted to your account. You have a potential overpayment	Refund

	credit because of these changes.	
CP25	We made changes to your return because we found a difference between the amount of estimated tax payments on your tax return and the amount we posted to your account. You're not due a refund nor do you owe an additional amount because of our changes. Your account balance is zero.	Zero Balance
LT26	You were previously asked information regarding the filing of your tax return for a specific tax period.	Information Request
ST26	Antes le pedían información referente a la manera que fue presentada su declaración de impuestos para un período tributario específico.	Solicitud de información
CP27	We've sent you this notice because our records indicate you may be eligible for the Earned Income Tax Credit (EITC), but didn't claim it on your tax return.	EITC
LT27	For us to consider an installment agreement for your overdue taxes, you must complete Form 433F, Collection Information Statement.	Installment Agreement

ST27	Para nosotros considerar establecerle un plan de pagos a plazos para sus impuestos vencidos, usted tiene que completar el Formulario 433F(SP), Declaración de Ingresos y Gastos.	Plan de pagos
CP30	We charged you a penalty for not pre-paying enough of your tax either by having taxes withheld from your income, or by making timely estimated tax payments.	Penalty
CP30A	We reduced or removed the penalty for underpayment of estimated tax reported on your tax return.	Penalty
CP32	We sent you a replacement refund check.	Refund
CP32A	Call us to request your refund check.	Refund
LT33	We received your payment; however, there's still an outstanding balance.	Balance Due
ST33	Recibimos su pago; sin embargo, todavía hay un saldo pendiente.	Saldo pendiente
CP39	We used a refund from your spouse or former spouse to pay your past due tax debt. You may still owe money.	Balance Due
LT39	We're required by law to remind you	Balance Due

	in writing about your overdue tax.	
ST39	La ley nos obliga a recordarle, por escrito, de su impuesto moroso.	Saldo pendiente
CP40	We are notifying you that we've assigned your tax account to a private collection agency for collection.	Information
LT40	We're trying to collect unpaid taxes from you. In order to do so, we may contact others to get or verify your contact information.	Balance Due
ST40	Tratamos de recaudar sus impuestos impagados. Para hacerlo, podemos comunicarnos con otras personas para conseguir o verificar su información de contacto.	Saldo pendiente
LT41	We're trying to collect unfiled returns from you. In order to do so, we may contact others to get or verify your contact information.	Balance Due
ST41	Tratamos de obtener las declaraciones que usted no ha presentado. Para hacerlo, podemos comunicarnos con otras personas para conseguir o verificar su información de contacto.	Saldo pendiente

CP42	The amount of your refund has changed because we used it to pay your spouse's past due tax debt.	Refund
CP44	There is a delay processing your refund because you may owe other federal taxes.	Balance Due
CP45	We were unable to apply your overpayment to your estimated tax as you requested.	Overpayment
LP47	We are requesting your assistance in locating a taxpayer that may or may not be currently employed by you.	Address Update
CP49	We sent you this notice to tell you we used all or part of your refund to pay a tax debt.	Overpayment
CP51A	We computed the tax on your Form 1040, 1040A or 1040EZ. You owe taxes.	Balance Due
CP51B	We computed the tax on your Form 1040, 1040A or 1040EZ. You owe taxes.	Balance Due
CP51C	We computed the tax on your Form 1040, 1040A or 1040EZ. You owe taxes.	Balance Due

CP52	We are informing the taxpayer a correction has been made to self-employment taxes claimed on Schedule SE, Form 1040.	Self-Employment Tax
CP53	We can't provide your refund through direct deposit, so we're sending you a refund check by mail.	Direct Deposit
CP53A	We tried to direct deposit your refund, but the financial institution couldn't process it. We are researching your account, but it will take 8 to 10 weeks to reissue your refund.	Direct Deposit
CP53B	We tried to direct deposit your refund, but the financial institution couldn't process it. We are researching your account, but it will take 8 to 10 weeks to complete our review and verify this refund.	Direct Deposit
CP53C	We tried to direct deposit your refund, but the financial institution couldn't process it. When refund payments are questionable, we review related returns to ensure the return is valid. We are researching your account, but it will take 8 to 10 weeks to complete our review and verify this refund.	Direct Deposit

CP53D	We can't direct deposit your refund because we limit the number of direct deposit refunds to the same bank account or on the same pre-paid debit card.	Direct Deposit
CP54B	Your tax return shows a different name and/or ID number from the information we have for your account. Please provide more information to us in order to receive your refund.	Name/SSN
CP54E	Your tax return shows a different name and/or ID number from the information we have for your account. Please provide the requested information.	Name/SSN
CP54G	Your tax return shows a different name and/or ID number from the information we have for your account. Please provide the requested information.	Name/SSN
CP54Q	Your tax return shows a different name and/or ID number from the information we have on file for you or from the information from the Social Security Administration (SSA).We previously sent you a notice asking you to provide us some updated information. We still haven't	Name/SSN

	received a response from you.	
CP59	We sent you this notice because we have no record that you filed your prior personal tax return or returns.	Filing
LP59	We previously sent you a notice of levy to collect money from the taxpayer named in the notice, but did not receive a response or an explanation of why you haven't sent it.	Levy
CP60	We removed a payment erroneously applied to your account.	Payment
LP60	We need information about a possible deceased taxpayer to help resolve a federal tax matter.	Information request
SP60	Necesitamos información sobre un posible contribuyente fallecido, para ayudarnos a resolver un asunto de contribuciones federales.	Solicitud de información
LP61	We need information about a taxpayer to assist us in resolving a federal tax matter.	Taxpayer Info Request
CP62	We applied a payment to your account.	Payment

LP62	We need information about a taxpayer to assist us in resolving a federal tax matter. We are asking for your help because we believe this person has an account with you.	Taxpayer Info Request
CP63	We are holding your refund because you have not filed one or more tax returns and we believe you will owe tax.	Refund
LP64	We are requesting your assistance in trying to locate a taxpayer that you may or may not know.	Locate Taxpayer
SP64	Con este aviso le solicitamos su ayuda para localizar a un contribuyente que usted puede o no conocer.	Localizar a un contribuyente
LP68	We released the notice of levy sent to you regarding the taxpayer named in the notice.	Levy
CP71	You received this notice to remind you of the amount you owe in tax, penalty and interest.	Balance Due
CP71A	You received this notice to remind you of the amount you owe in tax, penalty and interest.	Balance Due

CP71C	You received this notice to remind you of the amount you owe in tax, penalty and interest.	Balance Due
CP71D	You received this notice to remind you of the amount you owe in tax, penalty and interest.	Balance Due
CP71H	You received this notice to remind you of the amount you owe in tax, penalty and interest.	Balance Due
CP72	You may have claimed a frivolous position on your tax return. A frivolous return is identified when some information on the return has no basis in the law.	Frivolous Return
LT73	Your federal employment tax is still not paid. We issued a notice levy to collect your unpaid taxes.	Employment Tax
ST73	Aún no ha pagado sus impuestos federales sobre la nómina. Emitimos un aviso de embargo para recaudar sus impuestos impagados.	Impuestos sobre la nómina
CP74	You are recertified for EITC. You don't have to fill out Form 8862, Information To Claim Earned Income Tax Credit After Disallowance, in the future. You'll receive your EITC refund within 6 weeks as long as you	EITC

	don't owe other tax or debts we're required to collect.	
CP75	We're auditing your tax return and need documentation to verify the Earned Income Tax Credit (EITC) you claimed. The EITC and/or the Additional Child Tax Credit (ACTC) portions of your refund are being held pending the results of this audit. If you claimed the Premium Tax Credit (PTC), that portion of your refund is also being held.	EITC
LT75	Your federal tax is unpaid. We asked you to pay the tax, but haven't received your payment. We issued a notice of levy to collect your unpaid taxes.	Levy
ST75	Su impuesto federal no ha sido pagado. Le hemos solicitado que pague el impuesto, pero no hemos recibido su pago. Emitimos un aviso de embargo para cobrar sus impuestos sin pagar.	Aviso de embargo
CP75A	We're auditing your tax return and need documentation to verify the Earned Income Tax Credit (EITC), dependent exemption(s) and filing status you claimed.	EITC

CP75C	We're banned from claiming the Earned Income Tax Credit (EITC) in a prior tax year due to your intentional disregard of the rules or a fraudulent claim. Since your ban is still in effect, we disallowed the EITC for your current tax year.	EITC
CP75D	We're auditing your tax return and we need documentation to verify the income and withholding you reported on your tax return. This may affect your eligibility for the Earned Income Tax Credit (EITC), dependent exemption(s) and other refundable credits you claimed. We are holding your refund pending the results of the audit.	EITC
CP76	We are allowing your Earned Income Tax Credit as claimed on your tax return. You will receive any expected refund in 8 weeks provided you owe no other taxes or legal debts we are required to collect.	EITC
CP77	We are notifying you of our intent to levy certain assets for unpaid taxes. You have the right to a Collection Due Process hearing.	Levy
CP79	We denied the Earned Income Tax Credit (EITC) you claimed on your individual income tax return. You	EITC

	won't receive EITC with a qualifying child or children in the future until you prove your eligibility to receive it.	
CP79A	We denied all or part of the Earned Income Tax Credit (EITC) you claimed on your individual income tax return. We determined you recklessly or intentionally disregarded the EITC rules and regulations. For this reason, the law does not allow you to claim the EITC for the next 2 years.	EITC
CP79B	We denied all or part of the Earned Income Tax Credit (EITC) you claimed on your individual income tax return. We determined you made a fraudulent EITC claim. For this reason, the law does not allow you to claim the EITC for the next 10 years.	EITC
CP80	We credited payments and/or other credits to your tax account for the tax period shown on your notice. However, we haven't received your tax return.	Filing
CP81	We have not received your tax return for a specific tax year and the statute of limitations to claim a refund of your credit or payment for that tax	Filing

	year is about to expire.	
CP87A	We sent you this notice because we received a tax return from another taxpayer claiming a dependent or qualifying child with the same social security number as a dependent or qualifying child listed on your tax return. The last four digits of the social security number for each dependent or qualifying child we're concerned about is shown on the notice for your review.	Duplicate TIN
CP87B	We sent you this notice because you claimed an exemption for yourself and someone else also claimed you as a dependent exemption for the same tax year on another tax return. You can't claim an exemption for yourself if someone else is entitled to take an exemption for you as his or her dependent.	Duplicate TIN
CP87C	We sent you this notice because you claimed a dependent on your tax return with reported gross income for more than the amount of the exemption deduction. Someone else also claimed this dependent with the same social security number on another tax return. You can't claim someone whose gross income exceeds the deduction amount for a	Duplicate TIN

	dependent exemption unless that person is permanently and totally disabled at some time during the tax year and his or her income is from services performed at a sheltered workshop.	
CP87D	We sent you this notice because our records show you claimed someone as a dependent on your tax return who also filed a tax return with his or her spouse. Generally, you can't claim someone as a dependent who files a married filing joint tax return. In addition, someone who files a joint tax return usually doesn't fit the definition of a "qualifying child" for the Earned Income Tax Credit.	Duplicate TIN
CP88	We are holding your refund because you have not filed one or more tax returns and we believe you will owe tax.	Filing
CP90	We are notifying you of our intent to levy certain assets for unpaid taxes. You have the right to a Collection Due Process hearing.	Levy
CP90C	We levied your assets for unpaid taxes. You have the right to a Collection Due Process hearing.	Levy

CP91	We are notifying you of our intent to levy up to 15% of your social security benefits for unpaid taxes.	Levy
CP92	We levied your state tax refund for unpaid taxes. You have the right to a Collection Due Process hearing.	Levy
CP94	This notice is to inform you that a restitution-based assessment was made under Internal Revenue Code Section 6201(a)(4) in accordance with the court's restitution order. The amount due is based on the amount of restitution you were ordered to pay, as well as any other penalties and interest reflected on the billing summary.	Levy
CP301	We sent you this notice to inform that you visited IRS online services website and went through Identity Verification process.	Identity Theft
CP501	You have a balance due (money you owe the IRS) on one of your tax accounts.	Balance Due
CP501H	You have a balance due (money you owe the IRS) on your shared responsibility payment account.	ACA

CP503	We have not heard from you and you still have an unpaid balance on one of your tax accounts.	Balance Due
CP503H	You still have an unpaid balance on your shared responsibility payment account.	ACA
CP504	You have an unpaid amount due on your account. If you do not pay the amount due immediately, the IRS will seize (levy) your state income tax refund and apply it to pay the amount you owe.	Levy
CP508C	CP508C is sent when the IRS has identified your tax debt as meeting the definition of "seriously delinquent" and provided that information to the State Department. This could affect your passport.	Balance Due
CP508R	CP508R is sent when the IRS has reversed the certification of your tax debt as seriously delinquent, and notified the State Department of that reversal.	Balance Due
CP515I	This is a reminder notice that we still have no record that you filed your prior tax return or returns.	Filing

CP516	This is a reminder notice that we still have no record that you filed your prior tax return or returns.	Filing
CP518I	This is a final reminder notice that we still have no record that you filed your prior tax return(s).	Filing
CP521	This notice is to remind you that you have an installment agreement payment due. Please send your payment immediately.	Installment Agreement
CP522	We need financial information from you to determine the correct payment for your current installment agreement.	Installment Agreement
CP523	This notice informs you of our intent to terminate your installment agreement and seize (levy) your assets. You have defaulted on your agreement.	Levy
CP523H	This notice informs you of our intent to terminate your installment agreement.	ACA
CP547	We received your Form 2848, 8821, or 706, and we assigned you a Centralized Authorization File (CAF) number.	CAF

CP560A	Important Information about your child's Adoption Taxpayer Identification Number (ATIN). We assigned your child an ATIN.	Adoption TIN
CP560B	Important Information about your child's Adoption Taxpayer Identification Number (ATIN). We approved your request for a one-year extension.	Adoption TIN
CP561A	Important Information about your child's Adoption Taxpayer Identification Number (ATIN). Your child's ATIN expires in 3 months.	Adoption TIN
CP561B	Important Information about your child's Adoption Taxpayer Identification Number (ATIN). The extension for your child's ATIN expires in 3 months.	Adoption TIN
CP561C	Important Information about your child's Adoption Taxpayer Identification Number (ATIN). Your child's ATIN expired.	Adoption TIN
CP562A	Important Information about your Form W-7A, Application for Taxpayer Identification Number for Pending U.S. Adoptions. Your application was incomplete and we need more information to process	Adoption TIN

	your request for an ATIN.	
CP562C	Important Information about your child's Adoption Taxpayer Identification Number (ATIN). We need more information to process your one year extension request of your child's ATIN.	Adoption TIN
CP563	We reviewed your Form W-7A, Application for Taxpayer Identification Number for Pending U.S. Adoptions, and we need additional information in order to process it.	Adoption TIN
CP565	We gave you an Individual Taxpayer Identification Number (ITIN).	ITIN
CP565SP	Nosotros le asignamos un Número de Identificación Personal del Contribuyente (ITIN, por sus siglas en inglés).	ITIN
CP566	We need more information to process your application for an Individual Taxpayer Identification Number (ITIN). You may have sent us an incomplete form. You may have sent us the wrong documents.	ITIN
CP566	Necesitamos más información para tramitar su solicitud de un Número de	ITIN

(SP)	Identificación Personal del Contribuyente (*ITIN*, por sus siglas en inglés). Puede que nos haya enviado un formulario incompleto. Puede que nos haya enviado los documentos incorrectos.	
CP567	We rejected your application for an Individual Taxpayer Identification Number (ITIN). You may not be eligible for an ITIN. Your documents may be invalid. We may not have received a reply when we asked for more information.	ITIN
CP567 (SP)	Hemos denegado su solicitud para un Número de Identificación Personal del Contribuyente (*ITIN*, por sus siglas en inglés). Usted tal vez no reúna los requisitos para obtener un *ITIN*. Puede que sus documentos no sean válidos. Puede que no hayamos recibido su respuesta cuando le solicitamos más información.	ITIN
CP601	Usted tiene un saldo pendiente de pago (dinero que le debe al IRS) en una de sus cuentas contributivas.	Saldo pendiente
CP603	No hemos recibido respuesta de parte de usted y todavía tiene un saldo sin pagar en una de sus cuentas contributivas.	Saldo pendiente

CP604	Usted tiene un saldo sin pagar en su cuenta. De no pagar esta cantidad inmediatemente, el IRS embargará cualquier reembolso de impuestos estatales al que tenga derecho y aplicarlo al pago de su deuda.	Embargo
CP615I	Este aviso es un recordatorio, que según nuestros registros, todavía no tenemos información de que usted haya presentado su anterior declaración o declaraciones de impuestos.	Presentación de impuestos
CP616	Este es un recordatorio que todavía no tenemos un registro de que usted presentó su anterior declaración o declaraciones de impuestos.	Presentación de impuestos
CP618I	Lo presente, es el aviso final para recordarle que según nuestros registros, usted todavía no ha presentado su(s) declaración(es) anterior(es) de impuestos.	Presentación de impuestos
CP621	Este aviso es para notificarle que usted tiene un plan de pagos a plazos vencido. Por favor, envíe el pago inmediatamente.	Acuerdo de pagos a plazos
CP623	Este aviso es para informarle nuestra intención de cancelar su plan de pagos a plazos y confiscar (embargar)	Embargo

	sus bienes. Usted incumplió en su acuerdo.	
CP701B	Este aviso le comunica que el IRS necesita más información de usted para tramitar su declaración de impuestos con precisión.	Robo de identidad
CP701C	Enviamos el aviso CP701C a aquellos contribuyentes que actualmente no se ven afectados por el robo de identidad relacionado con los impuestos, para que reconozcan que han recibido los documentos estándares de robo de identidad y para informarles que su cuenta ha sido marcada con un indicador de robo de identidad.impuestos con precisión.	Robo de identidad
CP701E	Este aviso CP 701E se emite a los contribuyentes que pueden ser víctimas de robo de identidad, porque sus números de seguro social (*SSN*, por sus siglas en inglés) y posiblemente su información personal, se utilizaron para obtener el empleo, por alguien diferente al verdadero dueño del *SSN*.	Robo de identidad
CP701S	Recibimos su Formulario 14039 o una declaración similar para su reclamación de robo de identidad. Si se le adeuda un reembolso, lo	Robo de identidad

	emitiremos o nos comunicaremos con usted cuando se complete la tramitación de su caso o si necesitamos información adicional.	
CP711	Nosotros realizamos cambios a su planilla debido a que entendemos que hubo un cálculo erróneo. Como resultado de estos cambios, usted adeuda dinero por sus contribuciones.	Saldo pendiente
CP712	Hemos realizado cambios para corregir un error de cálculo en su planilla.	Error de cálculo
CP713	Hemos realizado cambios para corregir un error de cálculo en su planilla. No se le debe un reembolso y no adeuda una cantidad de dinero adicional a causa de estos cambios. El saldo de su cuenta es cero.	Saldo de su cuenta es cero
CP714	Le enviamos este aviso porque usted adeuda contribuciones pendientes de pago.	Saldo pendiente
CP721A	Hicimos el(los) cambio(s) que usted solicitó a su declaración de impuestos para el año tributario que aparece en su aviso. Como resultado de éste(estos) cambio(s) usted debe dinero en sus impuestos.	Saldo pendiente

CP721B	Hicimos el(los) cambio(s) que usted solicitó a su planilla de contribución para el año contributivo indicado en el aviso. Usted debe recibir su reintegro dentro de 2 a 3 semanas de su aviso.	Reintegro
CP721C	Hicimos el(los) cambio(s) que usted solicitó a su planilla de contribución, para el año contributivo indicado en el aviso. A usted no se le adeuda ningún reintegro, ni usted adeuda ninguna cantidad adicional. El saldo de su cuenta para este formulario de contribución y este año contributivo es cero.	Saldo de su cuenta es cero
CP721E	Como resultado de su auditoría reciente, hicimos cambios a su planilla de contribución para el año contributivo indicado en el aviso. Como resultado de estos cambios, usted adeuda dinero en sus contribuciones.	Saldo pendiente
CP721I	Hicimos cambios a su planilla de contribución para el año contributivo indicado en el aviso para las contribuciones de su Cuenta Individual de Ahorros para la Jubilación (*IRA*, por sus siglas en inglés). Usted adeuda dinero en sus contribuciones como resultado de	Saldo pendiente

	estos cambios.	
CP722A	Hicimos el(los) cambio(s) que usted solicitó a su declaración de impuestos para el año tributario que aparece en su aviso. Como resultado de éste(estos) cambio(s) usted debe dinero en sus impuestos.	Saldo pendiente
CP722E	Como resultado de su auditoría reciente, hicimos cambios a su planilla de contribución para el año contributivo indicado en el aviso. Usted adeuda dinero en sus contribuciones como resultado de estos cambios.	Saldo pendiente
CP722I	Hicimos cambios a su planilla de contribución para el año contributivo indicado en el aviso para las contribuciones de su Cuenta Individual de Ahorros para la Jubilación (*IRA*, por sus siglas en inglés). Usted adeuda dinero en sus contribuciones como resultado de estos cambios.	Saldo pendiente
CP740	Le informamos que hemos asignado su cuenta contributiva a una agencia privada de cobros para la recaudación.	Información
CP749	Le enviamos este aviso para	Pago

	informarle que hemos utilizado todo o parte de su reintegro para pagar una deuda contributiva.	
CP759	Le enviamos este aviso porque no tenemos registro que indique que usted radicó su planilla o planillas de contribuciones personales para uno o varios años anteriores.	Presentación de impuestos
CP771	Usted recibió este aviso para recordarle sobre la cantidad que adeuda en contribuciones, multas e intereses.	Saldo pendiente
CP772	Usted recibió este aviso para recordarle sobre la cantidad que adeuda en contribuciones, multas e intereses.	Saldo pendiente
CP773	Usted recibió este aviso para recordarle sobre la cantidad que adeuda en contribuciones, multas e intereses.	Saldo pendiente
CP774	Usted recibió este aviso para recordarle sobre la cantidad que adeuda en contribuciones, multas e intereses.	Saldo pendiente
CP2000	The income and/or payment information we have on file doesn't match the information you reported	Underreporter

	on your tax return. This could affect your tax return; it may cause an increase or decrease in your tax, or may not change it at all.	
CP2005	We accepted the information you sent us. We're not going to change your tax return. We've closed our review of it.	Underreporter
CP2006	We received your information. We'll look at it and let you know what we're going to do.	Underreporter
CP2057	You need to file an amended return. We've received information not reported on your tax return.	Underreporter
CP2501	You need to contact us. We've received information not reported on your tax return.	Underreporter
CP2566	We didn't receive your tax return. We have calculated your tax, penalty and interest based on wages and other income reported to us by employers, financial institutions and others.	ASFR
CP2566R	We previously sent you a CP63 notice informing you we are holding your refund until we receive one or more unfiled tax returns. Because we received no reply to our previous	ASFR

	notice, we have calculated your tax, penalty and interest based on wages and other income reported to us by employers, financial institutions and others.	
CP3219A	We've received information that is different from what you reported on your tax return. This may result in an increase or decrease in your tax. The notice explains how the amount was calculated and how you can challenge it in U.S. Tax Court.	Deficiency Notice
CP3219N	We didn't receive your tax return. We have calculated your tax, penalty and interest based on wages and other income reported to us by employers, financial institutions and others.	Deficiency Notice
Letter 0012C	Requesting information to reconcile Advance Payments of the Premium Tax Credit	Request for Information
Letter 0484C	Collection Information Statement Requested (Form 433F/433D); Inability to Pay/Transfer	Request for Information
Letter 0549C	Balance Due on Account is Paid	Balance Due

Letter 0681C	Proposal to Pay Accepted	Payment
Letter 0757C	Installment Privilege Terminated	Installment Agreement
Letter 1961C	Installment Agreement for Direct Debit 433-G	Installment Agreement
Letter 1962C	Installment Agreement Reply to Taxpayer	Installment Agreement
Letter 2257C	Balance Due Total to Taxpayer	Balance Due
Letter 2271C	Installment Agreement for Direct Debit Revisions	Installment Agreement
Letter 2272C	Installment Agreement Cannot be Considered	Installment Agreement
Letter 2273C	Installment Agreement Accepted: Terms Explained	Installment Agreement
Letter 2357C	Abatement of Penalties and Interest	Penalty
Letter 2603C	Installment Agreement Accepted - Notice of Federal Tax Lien Will be Filed	Installment Agreement

Letter 2604C	Pre-assessed Installment Agreement	Installment Agreement
Letter 2761C	Request for Combat Zone Service Dates	Request for Information
Letter 2789C	Taxpayer Response to Reminder of Balance Due	Balance Due
Letter 2800C	Incorrect Form W-4, Employee's Withholding Allowance Certificate	Withholding
Letter 2801C	Exempt Status May not be Allowed	Withholding
Letter 2802C	Your withholding doesn't comply with IRS guidelines	Withholding
Letter 2840C	CC IAPND Installment Agreement Confirmation	Penalty
Letter 3030C	Balance Due Explained:Tax/Interest Not Paid	Balance Due
Letter 3127C	Revision to Installment Agreement	Installment Agreement
Letter 3217C	Installment Agreement Accepted: Terms Explained	Installment Agreement

Letter 4281-A	Letter used for the Get Transcript incident to notify individuals whose SSNs were used to successfully access transcripts.	Identity Theft
Letter 4281-B	Letter used for the Get Transcript incident to notify individuals who had their SSN used unsuccessfully to obtain a transcript.	Identity Theft
Letter 4281-C	Letter used to notify potentially impacted individuals of an IRS data loss/inadvertent disclosure.	Identity Theft
Letter 4281-E	Letter used for the Get Transcript incident to notify the primary taxpayer on a tax return that the access may have included the social security numbers of others listed on the tax return and included language for protecting minors (under the age of 18).	Identity Theft
Letter 4281-F	Letter used for the Get Transcript incident to notify individuals who were indirectly related to the Get Transcript account (for example, spouse, alimony spouse, child care provider, dependent over the age of 18, etc.).	Identity Theft
Letter	Letter used for the Get Transcript incident to notify individuals whose	Identity Theft

	SSNs were used to successfully access transcripts and included language for protecting minors (under the age of 18).	
Letter 4310C	Someone may have attempted to impersonate you by using your name and Social Security number (SSN).	Identity Theft
Letter 4458C	We wrote to you because we didn't receive your monthly installment payment.	Installment Agreement
Letter 4883C	We received your federal income tax return; however, we need more information from you to process it.	Identity Theft
Letter 5071C	We received your federal income tax return; however, we need more information from you to process it.	Identity Theft
Letter 5447C	We received your federal income tax return, but we need more information to verify your identity in order to process your tax return accurately.	Identity Theft
Letter 5591	Advanced Premium Tax Credit recipients with no indication of return filing (non-filers) letter.	ACA
Letter 5591A	Advanced Premium Tax Credit recipients with no indication of return	ACA

	filing (non-filers) letter.	
Letter 5596	Advanced Premium Tax Credit recipients with no indication of return filing (non-filers) letter.	ACA
Letter 5598	You filed your 2014 federal tax return without reconciling advance premium tax credits and attaching a Form 8962, Premium Tax Credit.	ACA
Letter 5599	You filed your 2014 federal tax return without reconciling advance premium tax credits and attaching a Form 8962, Premium Tax Credit.	ACA
Letter 5600C	You may have reported owing too much Health Care Shared Responsibility Payment (SRP) on your 2014 income tax return.	ACA
Letter 5747C	We received your federal income tax return, but we need more information to verify your identity in order to process your tax return accurately.	Identity Theft
Letter 5821	You must renew your Individual Taxpayer Identification number (ITIN) to file your U.S. tax return.	ITIN

Letter 5821 (SP)	Usted debe renovar su Número de Identificación Personal del Contribuyente (ITIN) para poder presentar su declaración del impuesto estadounidense.	ITIN
Letter 5858	We received a copy of Form 1095-A for 2015. You must file your 2015 federal tax return with a Form 8962 to reconcile advanced premium tax credits.	ACA
Letter 5858 (SP)	Hemos recibido una copia del Formulario 1095-A de 2015. Usted tiene que presentar su declaración del impuesto federal de 2015 junto con el Formulario 8962, para conciliar los pagos por adelantado del crédito tributario de prima.	ACA
Letter 5862	We received a copy of Form 1095-A for 2015. You must file your 2015 federal tax return with a Form 8962 to reconcile advanced premium tax credits.	ACA

About The Author, About SFS Tax Problem Solutions

Jeffrey A. Schneider:

Jeffrey Schneider EA, CTRS, NTPI Fellow has the knowledge and expertise to help you reach a favorable outcome with the IRS. Whether you need assistance with reducing the amount of your tax debt, filing a back tax return or preparing a tax settlement by negotiating offers in compromise and filing installment agreements.

As an Enrolled Agent, Jeffrey Schneider is one of America's Tax Experts, who has earned the privilege of representing taxpayers before all administrative levels of the Internal Revenue Service.

He is a Fellow of the National Tax Practice Institute (NTPI), a Past President of the Florida Society of Enrolled Agents, the Palm Beach Chapter and Treasure Coast Chapter of the Florida Society of Enrolled Agents and a Director on the Board of the National Society of Enrolled Agents (NSEA). Schneider was recently appointed to the Internal Revenue Service Advisory Council (IRSAC).

SFS Tax Problem Solutions:

Providing tax and accounting services for more than 35 years to taxpayers just like you. SFS Tax Problem Solutions has saved their clients hundreds of thousands of dollars over the years.

Whether you need help with IRS or State Audits, Offer in Compromise, Appeals, Collections, Penalty and Interest Abatement, IRS Tax Liens and Levies, Wage Garnishments, Delinquent Taxes, or Tax Preparation, we have the expertise and experience to resolve all your tax problems.

Stay Connected with Jeffrey A. Schneider

http://nowwhathelp.com
http://sfstaxproblemsolutions.com/
http://igotataxnotice.com
Email: info@sfstaxacct.com

Made in the USA
San Bernardino, CA
19 February 2018